Praise for *Talk Yourself Happy*

"Kristi gets vulnerable and shares her heart with a healthy dose of humility and humor. I cried with her and laughed within the same page. Sometimes you think you need to have it all together but reading Kristi's testimony of how she let go and let God tak- ' o an even higher level was a spiritual shot in

—Sh   host

(for

"Common everyday happine   ... in an instant, especially when life comes at you hard. And I've seen Kristi Watts go through the hard times; first going through a divorce and eventual widowhood, then struggling to raise a child on her own, then leaving CBN and deciding to start her own ministry. The happiness that Kristi has found is not the common kind. She has found the happiness that heals, restores, and gives hope for the future; the happiness that comes from going through the hard times and coming out on the other side. In *Talk Yourself Happy*, Kristi shares her deeply personal journey of holding on to God's promises and then discovering that God's promises hold on to you."

—Gordon Robertson, CEO, the Christian
Broadcasting Network

"When you talk, speak God's words. If you do, you and those around you will gain an eternal perspective that will surpass your circumstances. As a teacher, counselor, and dad who has lost a child I know how important it is to speak the right words . . . and to receive them. This book is not a fluffy pep talk. It's a recalibration of you in relation to God. Get joy here."

—Ron Deal, speaker, therapist, and bestselling author
of *The Smart Stepfamily*

"*Talk Yourself Happy* is more like a conversation with a dear friend who knows where you really live. Kristi Watts keeps it real about the struggle to find a place called happy when life is making you otherwise. Practical, humorous, and honest, she gives convincing answers for the questions we ask in the midst of our pain."

—Michelle McKinney Hammond, TV host, speaker, and author of forty books, including *Get Over It and On with It*

"I highly recommend this book to anyone who is going through personal or professional struggles. It will not only encourage the reader to stand on the Word of God from day to day but will also strengthen them spiritually to face any challenge in the future. I recommend buying more than one copy and then gifting copies to anyone who may be facing life challenges."

—Dr. Shailja Collins (Ph.d Law), cofounder, Kingdom of Heaven Outreach

"Kristi and I have been friends for a long time. I have watched her walk through some of life's unexpected 'landmines' of hurt, loss, and disappointment. She has done it all with incredible grace and well-earned wisdom. While I love Kristi's humor and undeniable style, the quality I appreciate the most is her no-nonsense, honest to the bone, 'let's-be-real' attitude. She has a lot to say that is worth listening to, and she's right. The Word matters, and it can change our lives!! I *highly* recommend this book!"

—Terry Meeuwsen, cohost, *The 700 Club*; founder, Orphan's Promise

"Kristi has addressed the cry of countless numbers of people seeking answers to their frustrations, purpose for living, and spiritual confusion. This book gives practical direction in the midst of confusion, and instills hope in a heart of sadness. It ultimately leads the reader to a life transformed. For these reasons and others, it is a must read."

—M. Neville A. Smith, MBE, JP, FCMI, COKS; Bishop, International Fellowship of Christian Churches

talk
YOURSELF
happy

TRANSFORM YOUR HEART BY
SPEAKING GOD'S PROMISES

KRISTI WATTS

NELSON
BOOKS
An Imprint of Thomas Nelson

Published in Nashville, Tennessee, by Nelson Books, an imprint of Thomas Nelson. Nelson Books and Thomas Nelson are registered trademarks of HarperCollins Christian Publishing, Inc.

Thomas Nelson titles may be purchased in bulk for educational, business, fundraising, or sales promotional use. For information, please e-mail SpecialMarkets@ ThomasNelson.com.

Unless otherwise indicated, Scripture quotations are taken from the Holy Bible, New International Version®, NIV®. Copyright © 1973, 1978, 1984, 2011 by Biblica, Inc.™ Used by permission of Zondervan. All rights reserved worldwide. www. zondervan.com. The "NIV"and "New International Version" are trademarks registered in the United States Patent and Trademark Office by Biblica, Inc™

Scripture quotations marked ESV are taken from the ESV® Bible (The Holy Bible, English Standard Version®). Copyright © 2001 by Crossway, a publishing ministry of Good News Publishers. Used by permission. All rights reserved.

Scripture quotations marked NLV are taken from the New Life Version. © Christian Literature International.

Scripture quotations marked NKJV are taken from the New King James Version®. © 1982 by Thomas Nelson. Used by permission. All rights reserved.

Emphasis in Scripture references has been added by the author.

ISBN 978-0-7180-8384-7 (eBook)

Library of Congress Cataloging-in-Publication Data

Names: Watts, Kristi, 1971- author.
Title: Talk yourself happy : transform your heart by speaking God's promises / Kristi Watts.
Description: Nashville, Tennessee : Nelson Books, an imprint of Thomas Nelson, [2017]
Identifiers: LCCN 2016026037 | ISBN 9780718083861
Subjects: LCSH: God (Christianity)--Promises. | Self-talk--Religious aspects--Christianity. | Happiness--Religious aspects--Christianity.
Classification: LCC BT180.P7 W38 2017 | DDC 248.4--dc23 LC record available at https://lccn.loc.gov/2016026037

Printed in the United States of America

17 18 19 20 21 RRD 6 5 4 3 2 1

This book is dedicated to the love of my life.

My smile.

My heart.

My joy.

My happy.

My son.

Chase

Contents

CONTENTS

Introduction

It was January 1, and while the world celebrated a new year, all I could think was, *I can't believe I'm facing another year of nothing when all year I've been praying for something to happen.* This was officially year two of life without a job. Not an easy thing when you're a divorced, single parent whose spouse bailed on you and your son years prior, pillaging all bank accounts and leaving you high and dry to fend for yourself.

But it wasn't just the no-job thing or even the "God, have you noticed my bank account is on empty?" thing. It was the "What in the world is going on in my life?" thing. And the "Where did I go wrong?" thing. I didn't get it. I had done everything I knew to do, but I was quickly becoming heartsick and hope depleted. In the past, it was hope that had kept my engine of faith moving forward. But these days, my engine light was on and my hope in God was sputtering to a halt.

My life needed to change and I longed to be happy. In the Christian world, to say that you want to be happy is often met with a sideways glance and a frown. "To seek happiness is to seek something superficial, temporary, and circumstantial," I was told as I grew up in church. "It's not about being happy, it's about having the 'joy of the Lord.'"

I get it. I'm not going to argue. But I don't completely agree with that premise. I believe that happiness and joy are interrelated and completely dependent upon each other. David said, "In your presence there is fullness of joy" (Psalm 16:11 ESV). But what makes that joy full or complete? It's the *happy*.

The happy moments that come in the form of God taking action in our lives.

The kind of action that blesses, heals, helps, guides, loves, and restores.

The kind of action that collectively *fulfills* our lives and, as a result, brings us into his presence where there is *fullness* of joy.

It's all about those God moments. Those moments when you know . . . that you know . . . that you know that God is actively working with you and for you, because he loves you. I love those happy moments, because they continuously show us that God is trustworthy. One of my favorite scriptures is Proverbs 16:20: "Whoever *trusts* in the LORD, happy is he!" (NKJV).

Did you know that happiness is one of the many things God desires for us? In fact, the Greek word for "blessed" is *makarios*, which means "happy." There are more than twenty-seven verses in the Bible that mention happiness. If the Word of God is a reflection of the heart of God, and if we can see through his Word that God recognizes the importance of happiness in our lives, then I'm not one to argue with him. Bring it on!

The problem I was facing that January, though, was that no matter how hard I tried, I couldn't find the happy. I didn't know if I was blind to it or simply too marred from walking through the battlefield of life to see it. Whichever one it was, all evidence of what I knew to be happiness seemed to be gone.

It felt as if God's hand was so far away from me, I was beginning to believe that my God moments had become a thing of the past. So much so, I couldn't smile and I couldn't remember the last time I had laughed. My heart was so heavy that tears sprang up at the slightest mention of anything. I felt as if someone had injected my face with an overdose of Botox, and any expression of joy was restrained by the heaviness within my heart.

Did I do something wrong, God? I thought as I sat alone on my couch. *Are you angry with me?* I asked, not really expecting a response back. I had prayed and fasted so much in the past couple of years that I eventually told myself, *Why bother? There's nothing else I can say to God that I haven't said at least a million times over.* It felt as if my prayers were hitting the ceiling, and God had placed my life on the bottom of his to-do list. I felt alone in my struggle and was fully convinced that God had checked out, along with the rest of the world.

Here's the crazy part. In my arrogance, I felt that I deserved better. Sixteen years serving in Christian ministry should count for something, right? I had lived a good Christian life, so God was supposed to give me good! Wasn't that how life worked? You do good things, so you get good things? But my life didn't feel good. And I was in a genuine quandary as to how I had gotten to this place and, more important, how to get out.

I just wanted to be happy again.

As soon as the phone rang, I knew it was my mother. You

talk about a true woman of God; she is the real deal. My mother was the one who led me to the Lord when I was only five years old. As I sat on the couch in my family room remembering that day in my parents' bedroom, I quietly wished I could go back to the mind-set of that little girl.

Without hesitation or reserve, that little girl unabashedly placed her love and trust in the Lord. She talked to God all the time and could sense his presence in every aspect of her life. But now that girl was a full-grown woman with a suitcase full of life experiences that begged to stand in the way of fully trusting anyone. Even God.

"Happy New Year!" my mother said over the phone. "How are you doing today?"

My response was brief and stoic. I didn't have much to say.

She could sense my struggle, so she tried even harder to change my mood by sounding more upbeat and encouraging. It didn't work.

I wasn't in the mood to talk, but I muddled through the conversation anyway. The worries of life and the weight of discouragement had taken its toll. My mind inadvertently zoned in and out of the phone conversation until it was lured back at the mention of a struggle one of my sisters was going through. As I listened to my mother talk, my mind flashed back to when I had gone through a similar battle. But then my mind zoomed past the struggle and landed on the way God had responded and intervened.

I began to remember how God healed my broken heart when it felt as if it was shattered into a million pieces. I remembered how God supernaturally provided for me and my son with things only he knew we needed. And I remembered how God sent the right people at the right time to open the right doors for us.

Suddenly, now fully engaged in the conversation, I began to tell my mother what I had remembered. "If God did it for me, then he'll do it for her!" I said, with a new sense of rekindled hope in my voice as my words began to sink into my mind and change my heart.

The memory banks of God's goodness in both of our lives were unleashed. We couldn't stop talking about our personal experiences. "Remember when God did this . . . remember when God did that . . . !" we exclaimed, talking over each other. We were more than encouraged in the moment.

We were *recharged* by the hope we have in knowing who God is.

We were *renewed* by reminding ourselves of the vitality we gain by living in the presence of God.

And our personal circumstances were *redefined* because we chose to see our lives through the eyes of Christ rather than through the limitations of our own perspectives.

Our words were like lightbulbs illuminating the handprint of God within our lives. They revealed countless moments of rescue, blessing, healing, deliverance, help, comfort, and love. As I verbally recounted God's Word, God's promises, and God's hand on my own life, the weight that had been a suffocating force lifted like an early morning mist in the summer sun.

The smile that had evaded me for so long revealed itself once again.

I heard laughter. Not from afar, as I had grown accustomed to. It was close. It was familiar. It came from me. Basking in the sweetness of God's presence and grateful for the relief brought about by this welcomed breakthrough, I spoke words that would unveil my destiny.

"Girl, I just talked myself happy!"

Without skipping a beat, my mother responded, "Girl! I just talked myself happy too!"

That day, when I was speaking to my mother, something amazing happened. I realized that although my circumstances hadn't changed, my heart and perspective *had* changed. Once again I was able to see God—as in, see his active hand working in my life.

Even in the midst of one of the most challenging seasons, joy and happiness had reared their pretty little heads and I refused to let them go. I pursued them with a vengeance. And it was in that pursuit that I discovered the keys that bring us all to a place of everlasting joy and genuine happiness, the place where, no matter what we're going through in life, we *can* "talk ourselves happy."

So, how? How do we talk ourselves happy? Some may say this book's title is nothing more than a catchy motto with a feel-good tagline. Or that it's just another book filled with clichés and pep talks. But did you know that the concept of talking yourself happy is actually biblical?

To talk, to say, to speak the Word is a mandate found throughout the Bible. From the beginning when God *spoke* creation into existence, to the New Testament when God not only revealed his power *in* the spoken Word but *became* the spoken Word.

In the beginning was the Word, and the Word was with God, and the Word was God. (John 1:1)

The Word carries transforming power, and when we're *in* Jesus—the incarnate Word of God—we will find pure joy and happiness.

Joy is like a garden. Happiness is the flowers that make up the garden. And our words are what gives life to the flowers, allowing our happiness and joy to flourish and bringing us an immeasurable amount of pleasure. The words we speak have power to breathe life into our circumstances.

Good words, as in words that align with the Word of God, can turn an entire situation around. Words build our faith, transform our hearts, and change our perspectives, specifically when we see as God sees, speak as God speaks, and believe as God tells us to believe.

The purposeful act of aligning our words, our hearts, and our minds with God's Word—both Jesus himself and the Scriptures—is the key to happiness. Why? Because our words not only carry power—words *are* power! The ability to talk ourselves happy is a paradigm shift that will leave us transformed!

When we recognize the impact of our words and are intentional with them; when we choose to continuously speak words that reflect the heart and mind of Christ; when we remember God's blessings and verbally claim his promises, positive

THE PURPOSEFUL ACT
OF ALIGNING OUR
WORDS, OUR HEARTS,
AND OUR MINDS WITH
GOD'S WORD—BOTH
JESUS HIMSELF AND
THE SCRIPTURES—IS
THE KEY TO HAPPINESS.

thoughts are planted in our minds, which then affect the condition of our hearts and help us to live from a place of happiness.

If our words are rooted in the truth and come by way of the Word of God, then good will ultimately come forth. Not only will our lives be fed by the goodness found in the Word of God but our faith will be established and built up in the process! But on the flip side, when our words focus on our faulty perspectives of our circumstances, then it's inevitable that over time our own words will have a negative impact on our lives.

We'll be discouraged, discontent, and disheartened. Our words can derail our faith in God and cause a sense of hopelessness rather than happiness. What we do with our words has an impact, one way or the other.

A good man brings good things out of the good stored
up in his heart, and an evil man brings evil things out
of the evil stored up in his heart. For the mouth speaks
what the heart is full of. (Luke 6:45)

Another aspect of the power of our words is how they reveal what's in our hearts. Good, bad, ugly, or indifferent, our words are a direct reflection of the role we believe God plays in our lives. Our words reveal how much we *know* of God, and even the personal experiences we have *with* God.

Do the words you speak reveal the hope of God?
The healing power of God?
The deliverance of God?

The provision of God?

And the love of God?

Or do the words that you speak reveal a void where God might have been? Our words not only reveal how we perceive God but also how we think he perceives us. How do you think God sees you?

We must realize that our words are living and active. That's why words can create, build, define, heal, edify, free, protect, support, direct, and love. Words have the power to change. They can change your emotional state, your outlook, even your sense of hope. Words have power, but when the spoken word is backed by a person's personal belief system, as well as a mind-set based upon her knowledge, understanding, and experiences, then those words become like missiles shooting through the atmosphere and creating her destiny.

Are your words bringing forth life or death, blessings or curses?

In order to talk yourself happy, you have to recognize

1. The power of your words and the importance of being intentional and consistent with the words you speak.
2. The impact your words have on your perspective.
3. To have a right perspective or right understanding, you have to live right where God is.
4. Your words reflect what's in you. If you don't like what's coming out of you, then change what is in you by taking in the good of God's Word.

5. When your words are rooted in the truth of God's Word, they will act as a catalyst to transform your mind and heart to reflect the mind and heart of Jesus Christ.

Happiness is a choice. To live a life of happiness is to intentionally and continually speak words that align with the Word of God while allowing that Word to transform us in the process. In doing so, our faith in God will grow, and our thoughts will reflect God's goodness within our lives.

Words have impact, and when we use them to bless, heal, uplift, exhort, and speak the truth of God's Word in and over our lives, then we will suddenly realize we're talking ourselves happy—all day, every day, regardless of what life throws at us!

But here's the coolest part of all. God has so much more for us than happiness when we abide in him and speak words that reflect his heart. In this process of aligning ourselves with God, he unpacks more gifts of blessings that promise to transform our lives. Gifts such as hearts of compassion, the ability to forgive, walking in gratitude, and living in a place of hope that springs eternal—all blessings that naturally come during the pursuit of true happiness.

So if you're ready, it's time to take the journey and allow God to teach you how to talk yourself happy!

compassion

God Sees You. God Hears You. God Will Help You!

I stood at the entrance where the hallway opened up into our kitchen. I had just gotten off the phone with my parents who had informed me that they were driving to Virginia Beach to see us. Another eight-hour drive in less than twenty-four hours. I felt sorry for them. They had traveled over the weekend to talk with us, but my husband had been a no-show. He had disappeared—again.

With no apology or explanation for his disappearance, he was now standing in our kitchen fixing something to eat as if it was just another day. Up until this point my parents had elected to stay out of our marriage—which, by the way, was in a complete state of mayhem. But things had gotten so out of control they felt they had to step in.

"Your parents better not come here!" he shouted. "If they show up, I'm leaving!" He slammed the kitchen cabinets.

My parents had been present earlier when I discovered his collage of sticky notes on the kitchen counter with random and perplexing rants about life. The message that had pulled us all into a state of frenzy was the suicide note. Well, actually, a *threat* to commit suicide. Or a threat to *not* commit suicide. I'm not sure. Bottom line: when we read it, we all freaked out.

"I'm miserable," the note read. "The only thing that is keeping me alive is the thought of God and our son."

As soon as I read this, I had a flashback to a few weeks before, when I had come home from work to his calm announcement that "One day you're going to come home, and there's going to be blood splattered all over your pristine walls and your perfect house." He had been drunk. Again.

When we found the notes, I grabbed the phone and called all his friends, hoping that someone could tell me he was okay. Panic changed to anger when I reached the wife of one of his friends, who said, "Oh, yeah, your husband went with the boys to Bermuda for the weekend. He didn't tell you?"

"Nope. He didn't tell me," I fumed. The man who hadn't worked in more than a year—and spent his hours and money on the golf course rather than looking for a job—hadn't told me. The man who opted to scare the pee out of me with a kind-of-sort-of suicide note so that he could leave town and hang with the boys.

Yeah.

Nope.

He hadn't told me.

Crumbling the note in my fist, I shook my head in complete disgust. *He did it again,* I thought. I had fallen into his trap. It was a familiar formula: stir the waters to create a grand diversion, conjure up a case with as many lies as possible, and then manipulate all the players involved to ultimately gain what you want.

Welcome to my marriage.

"If you're not going to be here, then just tell me now so my parents don't have to drive another eight hours to get here!" I shouted while glaring at my husband.

My stress level was at an easy ten. I couldn't take his antics, lies, and threats another day. I was exhausted.

Turning to make a quick exit out of the kitchen, I felt a sharp pain in my abdomen. As I grabbed my stomach, a stream of warm liquid ran down my leg. I was six months pregnant. Hunching over and holding the bottom of my belly, as though to keep the baby from falling out, I ran up the stairs and locked myself in the bathroom.

I'm not sure why I didn't run to the phone to call my doctor. And I'm not sure why I went to the upstairs bathroom instead of the one downstairs. I guess I wanted to be as far away from my husband as possible. I dropped to the floor and curled into a ball, praying the baby would survive. To be honest, I'm not sure which baby I was referring to, me or the one growing inside.

Banging on the bathroom door, he yelled, now frantic. "Kristi, do you want me to call an ambulance? Do you want me to call the doctor?" Although he spoke loudly, it was as if his words were a million miles away.

I didn't respond. Not because I was angry with him; I was just tired. Tired of talking, tired of arguing and begging, and tired of the silent treatments. It was in that moment, lying on the cold bathroom floor, that I came to grips with the realization that the stress of this marriage on my mind, body, and spirit was too much to bear. I was done. The place within my heart that was initially warm, fuzzy, and filled with love for my husband had become a place that was cold, calloused, and closed off.

Think on those things that are lovely, honest, pure, and of good report, a small voice reminded me. I ignored it. I was too consumed with my own pain to think on anything other than how I felt. The truth was that I wanted to wallow in the pain, because I felt sorry for myself. Scene by scene, I hit replay on the movie reel within my mind, recollecting every negative event until I found myself lying in a cesspool of bitter emotions.

I remembered the time he told me, "I never loved you," after coming home from drinking one night. He'd thrown out those words as casually as one might throw out a "God bless you" after a sneeze. Although he apologized a few days later, I chose to hold on to those words, allowing them to solidify my case against my marriage.

Instead of agreeing with the Word of God, which told me to forgive, to walk in grace, and to extend mercy, I chose to agree with the words of a man who was clearly speaking out of his own pain. But I didn't care. I allowed his piercing words to define every aspect of our marriage. And how I defined our marriage was "irreparable" and "sabotaged" by the enemy who sat on the other side of the bathroom door.

I rested on that bathroom floor completely defeated. "Tell me what to do, Lord!" I cried out in desperation.

Pray for him.

Pray for who? I thought, suddenly sobering up from my meltdown.

Pray for him, I heard again. But the last thing I wanted to do was pray for the man I once called my greatest love but now branded as my greatest enemy.

Pray for your enemies, pray for those who persecute you and spitefully use you, I heard the small voice speak again.

I didn't want to. I had spent countless days and nights praying for this man and our marriage, and I didn't have the mental strength to pray for either anymore. After all, I told myself, if I did pray, I wouldn't mean it anyway. But then, not knowing what else to do, I hoisted myself up from the floor, pressing my back against the bathroom cabinet, and prayed. It took everything in me, but I forced my mouth to form words that lifted up the man I felt used his own words to tear me down.

Two words. At first, that's all I could muster. Two-word prayers. "Help him. Heal him. Deliver him. Save him."

As the engine of a car warms up with the start of an ignition, so the spoken Word of God warmed up my heart as I prayed. At first it was a struggle. I mean a *real* struggle. In that moment I didn't like my husband, and I found it very difficult to pray for someone I didn't like. The only words circling my mind were far from appropriate when speaking with the Lord. Rather than using my own words, I chose to recite scriptures, to speak God's Word back to God.

"Lord, you said that 'no weapon formed against us shall prosper.' Yet it seems like an entire army is against our marriage. So, Lord, I'm asking that you step in and heal him. Heal us, Lord."

God's Word began to chisel off the hardened areas of my heart that were forever trying to grow back. All night long I prayed for that man, our baby, and our marriage. I had no clue what was going to be on the other side of the bathroom door when I opened it later, but I knew one thing: I was going to trust God with everything, no matter the outcome.

I'm not sure when or even how it happened, but during those hours spent praying on the bathroom floor, an incredible peace came over me. In that peace I heard the Lord speak to my heart, "The baby is going to be fine and so are you." But something else significant happened. A major shift. As I cried out to God on that bathroom floor and recited his Word, I began to recognize how my own words often contradicted God's.

"Lord, heal my marriage," I would pray time and time again. But then, while talking to a girlfriend, I would say, "Nothing can help our marriage. Our marriage is doomed. I don't even know if I want to be married anymore."

Other times I would pray, "Lord, heal his heart and deliver my husband from everything that's holding him back in life. Change him back into the man I married." But then later on I would say, "He is who he is, and he's never going to change."

Speaking God's Word is like igniting a flame that transforms the darkness into light. Yet, every time I used my own words to contradict the Word of God and the promises of God, it was like pouring a bucket of water on that flame. My negative and contradictory words extinguished the light, creating a pile of soot and ash dampening my faith.

God tells us, "The tongue has the power of life and death,

SPEAKING

GOD'S WORD IS

LIKE IGNITING

A FLAME THAT

TRANSFORMS

THE DARKNESS

INTO LIGHT.

and those who love it will eat its fruit" (Proverbs 18:21). That night was the beginning of my understanding the impact of my words. I began to understand how—without even realizing it—I was speaking death more often than life into my marriage.

That night I committed to change. I was going to speak life into my husband. Life into my marriage. And life into every situation by not only speaking the Word of God, but depending on the Word to help me right where I was.

The next morning, not having slept a wink, I walked out of the bathroom, got dressed, and appeared at my job as a cohost on *The 700 Club*. With a renewed sense of peace and the prospect of hope returning to my heart, I felt confident enough to face my marriage another day.

Unfortunately, three months later, shortly after our son was born, my husband performed his final disappearing act and abandoned us for good. Even though I suffered from a battered heart and a pillaged bank account, secretly I was relieved. But the prospect of raising a newborn on my own, with no support from my husband—financially, emotionally, physically, or mentally—was definitely a challenge. Nevertheless, God would prove himself faithful in my life. I would begin to learn that true happiness wasn't contingent upon the *who*s in my life, but rather the *what*s.

What was God doing?

What did God want me to learn?

And what were the promises of God for my life that would restore my hope and bring happiness back into my soul?

"Chase, hurry up and get downstairs. You don't want to miss the bus!" I yelled from the kitchen.

Man, I love this kid, I thought as I finished packing his lunch. *He's only eleven years old, but he's absolutely brilliant, with a genuine heart for God.*

"I'm coming," he said, while trotting down the stairs.

With lunch box in hand, I followed him out the back door and walked alongside him, praying out loud for his day. "Lord, thank you for giving Chase the mind of Christ. Lord, help him to make wise decisions and be a godly example of your love today."

I didn't care that I was standing at the end of my driveway still in my bathrobe and head scarf that I wore at night. I didn't give a second thought to the prospect that neighbors heard me praying out loud for my son. Through the years, prayer had become my bedrock and Jesus my one consistent friend.

Even though I grew up in a Christian home and had accepted Christ into my heart at five years old, it was the breakdown of my marriage that catapulted me into a deep relationship with Christ. I pursued the Lord the way my mother pursued a 50-percent-off sale.

It was the Holy Spirit who kept me sane during those years struggling as a single mom.

It was the Word of God that gave me hope to press on to another day.

And it was Jesus' unfailing love that freed me from every offense and every offender.

I waved good-bye and turned to walk back into the house. I had nowhere to go. Not that I was counting, but it had been a year, four months, and twenty-two days since I had left CBN, and I was waiting for the Lord to give me an open door. So far, nothing.

At that point, I had tapped every contact I knew in the television world. I had searched every job site on the Internet and built a fabulous résumé reel, highlighting an impressive career in television spanning more than twenty years. And yet, not one callback, not one interview, not even a rejection letter. Nothing.

"Crickets," as one friend says. "It's the sound you hear when you ask people for help, and they don't respond."

I had reluctantly filed for unemployment, which made me feel like a failure. It is especially humbling when you've completed the top tier of schooling and held a high-profile position for several decades. When you've been the one people contact to get ahead in life and now those you've helped don't return your phone calls—let's just say, it hurts.

One requirement to receive unemployment is that you have to apply for at least two jobs a week. I wasn't sure there were any more jobs to apply for, but I pressed on. Television wasn't opening its doors to me, so I ventured out and applied for teaching jobs, writing jobs, and was on the cusp of applying for babysitting jobs.

My sister informed me, however, that babysitting should be my last resort, since I didn't really have patience for kids. "Not all kids," I reminded her. "Just the disrespectful, undisciplined, somebody-needs-to-slap-some-sense-into-them kind of kids." She just rolled her eyes.

I needed a job. *I'm doing everything I know to do, and nothing is working,* I thought.

"Lord, you said to trust you." But nothing.

"Lord, you said to have faith in you." I did, but nothing.

"Lord, you said to pray to you." But nothing.

I was at a complete loss. I'd always prided myself on being the good Christian girl who made all the right decisions, and now, as if I was trying to please a parent, I reminded God of all my good deeds just in case he had forgotten. "Lord, I've been teaching a weekly Bible study. I've reached out into the community to volunteer. I spend my days reading and studying the Bible. Shouldn't these things count for something?" I asked.

Crickets.

What frustrated me the most was praying for others to have the same things I was praying for myself and watching God answer my prayers for them but not for me. An acquaintance of mine wanted to move, so I prayed the Lord would act swiftly on her behalf and send a buyer to her home. Meanwhile, my house was all boxed up and still waiting for the moving truck along with the new job. Within a few months, she was moved and gone. I was opening boxes looking for the curling iron I had packed months before.

It was time to have a real talk with Jesus to get some answers. Convinced my prayers were hitting the ceiling, I ventured out to a place where I knew God would hear me. I grabbed my Bible, a folding chair, and a couple of blankets. I was headed to my Mount Sinai: the beach. It was where I always expected to hear God's voice through the crashing of the waves.

It was a gorgeous day, not a cloud in the sky, but it was freezing cold. I didn't care. I wasn't leaving until I heard from God. Period. I lugged my beach chair and blanket through the sand while clutching my Bible. I positioned myself right on the edge of the ocean, close enough to taste the salt and feel light sprays of water on my face with each crashing wave. My strategy was to go extra holy in my prayers. I was ready to recite every scripture back to God as if that was the secret code to get him to do something. I was prepared to declare and decree and proclaim the Word over my life.

But inexplicably, when I opened my mouth, I turned into a three-year-old and proceeded to howl like a baby. My words stammered out, and I started to do one of those hiccup cries where every word comes out disjointed.

"L-o-o-r-d. W-h-a-t—is—g-o-ing ooooooooooon?" I blubbered.

"Why a-r-e yooooouu ignorinnnng meeeeee!!?" I wailed.

I was a complete basket case.

When I finally composed myself enough to form slightly more thoughtful sentences, I couldn't stop myself. I had complete diarrhea of the mouth, and like a machine gun I just started shooting out questions at God. "Tell me what I need to do. Did I do something wrong, Lord? Have I failed you in some way? Do I need to pray more? Fast more? Lord, are you angry with me? Did I miss something? Lord, what is it? Please, just tell me. Just tell me something. *Anything!*"

Crickets.

Wiping the tears from my face, I looked out into the ocean and strained to see as far as I could see. It really was a beautiful sight. But all I kept thinking was, *Lord, you can create the heavens and the earth, the seas and every living thing in there, and you can't give me a job?*

Then, as if the rolling waves delivered the word to my feet, the Lord spoke: "Compassion."

I froze. One slight bit of movement might make God stop talking to me, I thought.

I waited.

And waited.

Then waited some more.

When I couldn't wait anymore, I just said, "Compassion for what, Lord?"

Nothing. Not another word. So I picked up my Bible.

As if I had just received a critical clue to solving a mystery, I flipped to the back of my Bible in search of the concordance. I scanned through the scriptures under the section marked *compassion*. I couldn't concentrate at first, because my eyes kept darting back and forth, attempting to take in all the scriptures at once.

"Kristi, slow down. Get a grip," I told myself.

Then my eyes fell on Psalm 78:38. I flipped to the passage to read the entire chapter and get the full picture of what God was saying. In Psalm 78, the author recounts the story of the Israelites who were delivered from a place of slavery and ushered into their promised land. The problem was that while in the place of transition ("the wilderness"), the promise was delayed. A journey that should have taken only eleven days lasted forty years! Why?

The general thought is that their murmuring and complaining toward God delayed the promise. Their own words reflected what was in their hearts and minds: disbelief.

With their words:

they flattered Him [God] with their mouth,
And they lied to Him with their tongue;
For their heart was not steadfast with Him.
(PSALM 78:36–37 NKJV)

With their minds, they:

forgot His works
And His wonders that He had shown them.
(PSALM 78:11 NKJV)

Because they *did not believe* in God,
And did not trust in His salvation.
(PSALM 78:22 NKJV)

With their hearts:

they sinned even more against Him
By rebelling against the Most High in the wilderness.
And they *tested God in their heart*
By asking for the food of their fancy.
(PSALM 78:17–18 NKJV)

The bottom line was that they didn't believe God would do what he said he was going to do—even though God had already proven himself by performing countless miracles in their lives.

The more verses I read in Psalm 78, the more my heart sank.

"Are you trying to tell me something, God?" I asked sheepishly.

I felt condemned, because I aligned my attitude with those of the Israelites. *Was God angry with me for not being a stronger Christian? Was I testing God by making my faith contingent upon his giving me my heart's desire? Was I provoking him like the Israelites did?* I wondered.

All I could focus on was the word *they* in those verses. My eyes could only see the fragility of man rather than the power of God. I didn't realize that God wasn't expressing his anger toward me because I questioned him and my situation, but rather, God was trying to guide me to embrace *his response* to their frailties.

"Kristi, read Psalm 78:38!"

> But He, being *full of compassion, forgave* their iniquity,
> And did not destroy them.
> Yes, many a time He turned His anger away,
> And did not stir up all His wrath;
> For He remembered that they were but flesh.
> (PSALM 78:38–39 NKJV)

God's response was compassion, not condemnation! The word *compassion* means to suffer with another and to have a strong desire to alleviate that suffering. God wasn't standing above me with folded arms ready to punish me; he was standing alongside me, embracing me, sharing in my pain. God knew that I was struggling in the wait.

He knew that although my mouth spoke praises, my heart was quietly faltering.

He knew that as each day passed, my grip on my faith was getting looser and looser.

But God wasn't angry with me. No! He had sympathy toward me. And not just sympathy alone. He wanted to do something about it!

My eyes were drawn to the phrase "full of compassion." *Full.* I mulled it over. God's sympathy for his children runs deep. It's not a fleeting moment of emotion nor a passing response. The revelation that God knew my pain and had the power—and the desire—to alleviate that pain warmed my wavering heart despite the cold sea breeze.

God was teaching me that his love for his children is greater than any of us could possibly imagine. His love trumps the fears we may have of falling short as Christians.

For years I had told myself that if I wasn't the perfect Christian or in some way wavered in my faith, God would be angry with me. I would even go so far as telling myself that, because of my own failures, God was justified in punishing me or withholding his goodness from me. But I was believing and speaking a lie.

The truth of God's Word says, "The LORD is good to all, and His tender mercies are over all His works" (Psalm 145:9 NKJV).

God was working on my behalf; I just needed to see it.

God was fulfilling his promise that he would never leave or abandon me. Even though I couldn't see the outcome yet, he was right there blessing me along the way, revealing his handprint on my life. And just being able to recognize God's hand was bringing me a level of happiness.

God's compassion was like a balm to my hurting soul, even more so as I meditated on his words and repeated them to myself. But compassion—true compassion—can't stop at receiving from the Lord. When it truly changes you, it can't help but multiply, and your words of mercy, love, and help toward others will reflect that. And your actions will follow suit.

———

"Go knock on those people's door, and pray with them," I heard the Lord say to me.

Come on, Lord. I barely know them, I sighed. *How weird will that be?*

I was walking my little five-pound puppy around my neighborhood when the Lord spoke to my heart. I wanted to pretend that I didn't really hear him. It's one thing to pray for people when they ask you, but it's another when you knock on someone's door unannounced and uninvited. It's so uncomfortable.

I heaved a deep sigh. I knew I had to do it. It's not as if they were strangers to me. After all, my son played outside with their son.

I ran up to the door, rang the doorbell, and waited about 2.3 seconds before I hustled back down the driveway, dragging my puppy behind me, thinking, *Well, I guess they're not home.*

The next day, while walking my dog again, I saw a car parked in that same driveway. Again I heard, "Go knock on their door, and pray for them."

I knocked maybe two times before the door opened and a

COMPASSION—

TRUE COMPASSION—

CAN'T STOP

AT RECEIVING

FROM THE LORD.

stocky man stepped out on the front porch. He gave me a weary smile and said, "Hi." His eyes revealed the story of someone in deep pain.

Before I lost my nerve I said, "I know this sounds strange, but I was wondering if I could pray with you."

"Yes. Please," he said as if he had been waiting for the request.

I reached out to touch the top of his arm out of sheer habit, then caught myself and said, "Is it okay if I touch your arm?"

"Of course," he said.

Before I closed my eyes, the presence of the Holy Spirit fell on that front stoop, and words flowed out of my mouth. The words the Lord spoke through me were like arrows shooting right into this man's heart, delivering a healing salve to his soul.

When I stopped praying and opened my eyes, I saw a man completely overcome by the power of the Lord. His face was saturated with tears. Although you could tell that a huge weight had been lifted off of him, his body still slumped from the blanket of compassion the Lord had placed on him.

"That was the most beautiful prayer I've ever heard in my life," he said softly, trying to conceal the tears that were still streaming from his eyes. Wiping his face, he briefly shared some personal challenges he was facing.

My heart hurt for him. I quietly listened and let him talk. He needed to talk.

When he paused for a moment, I gently spoke of Christ's love for him. I recounted a bit of my own love story with the Lord and talked about how the Lord loved me through my pain.

"I've tried praying before but always felt that God didn't care enough to listen to me," he sniffled. "For the past few days, I was sitting in my house praying to God, asking him to show me a sign that he heard me." His voice quivered. "He heard me. God heard me," he repeated, unable to hold back the sobs.

By now my eyes were burning with tears too. I gave him a brief hug, then walked away. My heart was so happy. It was amazing to witness God's love for this man who, by his own admission, didn't have a relationship with God, yet was able to experience the fullness of him because he was open to receive him. God used the words of my mouth to speak to his son's heart, and those words of encouragement ignited a hope inside of him.

It's amazing how we can pass people on a daily basis and choose not to acknowledge the hurt we see in their eyes. We see it; we just don't feel like doing anything about it. We feel too overwhelmed with our own burdens, so the prayers that come out of our mouths are dominated by what's going on in our lives, what we want to see happen for us.

The hard truth I came to realize was that I had been so consumed with my own needs that I had failed to see the needs of those around me. I'm not talking about the needs of random strangers; I'm talking about the friends, family, and neighbors I talked to every day but never took the time to *really* see.

During the next few weeks, I recognized how the Lord was gently removing me from being stuck in front of the mirror and was guiding me to the window, allowing me not only to see the struggle of others but also to do something about it. The Word was coming to life by bringing life to others through action.

While I was still asking God for a job and waiting for him

to open a door, I was starting to realize that he *was* opening up doors all around me. Maybe not doors that contributed to my bank account, but definitely doors that pointed me toward others and blessed me with treasures beyond the dollar.

Treasures such as an increasing faith in the things of God.

A tender heart of compassion to see and help those I normally was blind to.

And a growing sense of joy that was brought about by those God-moments that made me happy.

One time, my sister was burdened by a major presentation for work. Instead of just acting as a sounding board for her, I offered to help her with it. You would have thought I had offered her a million dollars.

On another occasion, a single mom trying to balance full-time work and full-time parenting was overwhelmed trying to fix up her house, so I put on some old clothes, grabbed a bucket of cleaning supplies, and headed over. When she opened the door, she stared at me as though I were Ed McMahon announcing she had won the Publishers Clearing House sweepstakes. With our kids at school and the music blaring, we cleaned her house together with a vengeance. We painted walls, washed windows, and dusted light fixtures. It was fun.

"Thank you so much for helping me," she said.

"My pleasure. None of us can do life alone. We all need help," I said, smiling as I inadvertently pressed my arm against the freshly painted walls.

Laughing at my clumsiness while recognizing the open door, I shared all the ways God had helped me as a single parent. I told her that in spite of countless setbacks and challenges, the Lord had always provided for Chase and me.

"He not only met all our needs but has been the One who filled the void that my ex-husband left," I said, knowing that she, too, struggled in that department. My words of empathy and compassion unlocked something within her heart, and before long she also began to talk about the goodness of God in her own life. Good moments that she had neglected to see at the time but was now remembering sparked a transformation in her countenance.

She was *talking herself happy*, and it was so cool to witness. Cleaning, laughing, and exchanging stories of God's goodness completely transformed the atmosphere of her home from a place of tension to a place of joyous praise. We both concluded that if God helped us before, he would help us again, because God is faithful, even when we're not.

It was easy to feel sympathy toward someone I liked and felt deserved help. It was completely different, however, when the person in front of me was someone who had hurt me. Let's be real. Compassion can seem like mission impossible when God points to someone we don't feel deserves our sympathy. Let alone, our help. But true compassion is the ability to look beyond the offense and the offender and see the heart of the issue through God's eyes.

God's response to the Israelites, who tested God at every turn, was completely opposite of what most of us would have done. "He turned His anger away" and acknowledged that "they were but flesh" (Psalm 78:38–39 NKJV). True compassion comes out of a place of love. When we have God's love within our hearts, then we will have hearts of compassion. Even when the person God requires us to embrace is the person who caused us the most pain.

As soon as I hit "play" on the answering machine I recognized the voice. It was my ex-husband. The man who had abandoned me and my son eleven years earlier. I hadn't heard from him in years. When he'd left, he'd left us for good.

I was in no hurry to return his call. The very sound of his voice set off a firestorm of bad memories. I took a deep breath. Then, like a light switch, I turned off the temptation to entertain negative thoughts. "Whatever things are pure, whatever things are lovely, whatever things are of good report, meditate on these things," I said out loud (Philippians 4:8 NKJV).

Through the years, I had trained myself to squelch negative thoughts that tried to fester in my mind. Every time a bad memory surfaced, I quoted Scripture out loud. When my husband first left us, I found myself reliving hellish moments in our marriage over and over again in my mind. I worked myself up into a frenzy every time and got sad, angry, and hurt all over again. It seemed as though I needed healing and deliverance every day. The only way I could get the thoughts to stop badgering me was by speaking the Word of God out loud.

"Take every thought captive," I would remind myself (2 Corinthians 10:5 ESV).

"Lord, you said I have the mind of Christ and I know your

TRUE COMPASSION
IS THE ABILITY TO
LOOK BEYOND THE
OFFENSE AND THE
OFFENDER AND SEE
THE HEART OF THE
ISSUE THROUGH
GOD'S EYES.

mind is full of peace, so give me your mind, Lord, because I need some peace today," I pleaded. And he did.

I had forgiven my ex-husband years before. In fact, one of the few times that I'd seen him since he left was a time I flew to where he was just to tell him that I had forgiven him and to ask his forgiveness in return. Actually, I should have thanked him for all those awful years, because it was living in that place of crazy that drove me into the arms of my heavenly Father.

I waited a day before I called him back.

"Kristi," he answered.

"Yes, I received your message. How may I help you?" I replied formally.

Bypassing all pleasantries he said, "I have stage-four cancer of the esophagus, and the doctors have given me only a couple of months to live."

Many people might have dropped to their knees and wailed into the phone at such news, but my response was far from that. "Really. When did you find out?" I said, as if he had told me that he had a common cold.

He had lied to me for so many years that I instinctively assumed he was lying about this too. Yes, even about cancer. He didn't have much else to say, so he hung up the phone. Probably baffled by my stoic response.

It was such a strange feeling. The man I had exchanged vows with seventeen years earlier, I now had no attachment to whatsoever. I was amazed at how much easier it was to have compassion toward a complete stranger or an acquaintance than toward someone I had once loved who had hurt me.

I e-mailed one of his old college friends just in case he was telling me the truth. The reply came quickly. "Yes, Kristi, sadly it's true."

I called my ex-husband back.

"I'm sorry. I didn't mean to sound so callous. To be honest, I didn't believe you. How are you doing?" I now asked, genuinely concerned.

I could tell he was tired of hearing that question and even more tired of answering it.

"I'm fine," he said.

Then after a long pause he mumbled, "Can I come see you and Chase?" This would be the first time he would meet his son. Actually, he had seen him as a baby, but I don't think that counts.

"Okay," I said, not sure what else to say. The door had always been open for him to see his son; he had just chosen not to. I was not about to shut the door on him now.

Of course, I was a little freaked out. All I could think about was what impact this would have on Chase. Not just the meeting-your-father-for-the-first-time kind of impact, but the your-father-who-you-just-met-is-dying-of-cancer kind of impact. Now what?

I needed to lie down.

I talked to my ex-husband more in the following weeks than I had during the past eleven years. He explained that the tumor was in his esophagus, which prevented him from eating or drinking. So the doctors had installed a feeding tube into his stomach.

"My second round of chemo should be complete after Thanksgiving, so I'd like to come see you guys then," he said.

"Okay," I replied.

Here's where it gets real. I didn't want to see him. Not because of the cancer, but because, after all these years, why? This man carried with him a basket of drama wherever he went, and I didn't want it back in my life. When he first left, I wanted him to have a relationship with Chase just because I thought every son needed his father. But through the years, I realized that his absence was a blessing and God had stepped in where a man had stepped out.

"I am a father to the fatherless and a protector to the widow" (Psalm 68:5, author's paraphrase), the Lord spoke to my heart one night.

I'll never forget that moment as long as I live. I was holding my baby boy in my arms, panicked about how I was going to raise a son alone. God soothed my soul when he made me that promise. And from that moment to this day, God has been faithful to his Word. He's taken care of my son like a father and taken care of me like a husband.

"Lord, shut the door. Keep him from getting on that plane," I quietly begged.

I didn't know what to expect. This man was now a complete stranger to us. When he walked out of our home, he chose to keep his life a secret from us. I didn't know where he lived or what he did, who he was with, or what lifestyle he led. Every couple of years, I would hear secondhand reports of something he was up to, but other than that, nothing.

"I'm here in Virginia Beach. It's late. I'll meet up with you guys tomorrow," the text read.

I didn't sleep all night.

"Jesus, help me to handle this situation wisely," I prayed. "Protect Chase and me." From what? I didn't know. The unknown was freaking me out.

He was an hour late meeting us at the restaurant. I had already prepped my son on what to expect from his father's physical appearance. I knew he had lost a significant amount of weight, but, good Lord, I was shocked. His five-foot-nine-inch frame that had once carried approximately 180 pounds was down to 108 pounds. His head was bald from the chemo, and he dragged his feet as he walked. Each step he took was clearly labored. As soon as I saw him walking toward our table, I leapt to my feet and raced toward him. I gave him a big hug, making sure not to squeeze him so hard as to hurt him.

He carried with him three small gift bags: one for Chase, one for me, and one for my little five-pound puppy. I grabbed the bags as he slid into the booth. Every movement took effort. I could see that he was determined to conceal the pain he felt in his chest.

"It feels like a sharp knife is stabbing me nonstop. I'm in constant pain," he had confided during one of our earlier phone calls.

He sat directly across from Chase. His eyes refused to blink.

"He looks just like me," he said in amazement.

"I can't stop looking at him," he said to no one in particular.

Chase just grinned from ear to ear looking back at him. I couldn't stop smiling either. Chase kept looking at his father, his father kept looking at him, and I kept watching them both. The evening went beautifully. My ex-husband had the waiter bring out a birthday dessert even though it wasn't Chase's birthday.

"This is for all the birthdays I missed," he said sheepishly.

"It's all good," I said, smiling at him.

Compassion. It was creeping up in me, and I didn't even know it.

The next day, while Chase was in school, my ex-husband wanted to meet for coffee. After fifteen minutes, I called his phone to see where he was. He answered, clearly confused. His words were slurred, and he was talking painfully slowly.

"Are you okay?" I asked. "Where are you?"

He had gone to the wrong coffee shop. The normally sharp man was discombobulated. When he arrived at the right coffee shop, he laid his head on the table. Exhausted.

I couldn't take it anymore. I jumped up and said, "Come on!"

Initially, I had no intention of taking him to my home. It was a place I had established as off limits. Our home was our refuge, our safe place, and I was careful who I allowed to enter it. I had fought so hard to keep the drama out that I refused to allow anyone to bring it back in.

But now I put my arms around the man who had once broken my heart and walked with him to the car. When we got to the house, I led him to the brown leather chair we had bought together years before. He was shivering. It wasn't cold to me, but I guess when you have barely any body fat, you're going to get cold. I quickly grabbed a blanket and threw it in the dryer to heat it up.

Then I snatched a bucket from the garage. It was an uncomfortable thing to witness, but he threw up every couple of minutes. His tumor completely blocked his esophagus passageway, so he even spit up his saliva.

He was constantly thirsty, so I brought him some water. He would drink some, but within seconds he was heaving it back up. The sound echoed in the bucket, which made it even tougher to listen to. I tried with everything in me not to react, but the sound alone made me want to throw up as well.

And suddenly, there it was. Compassion. Full blown and spilling over. I didn't care about what had been done in the past. All I saw was a man suffering, and my heart longed to help him.

As I sat massaging his ice-cold hands and arms, I couldn't help but think of the man I had married—before the alcohol and the fights.

I talked about the fun memories we'd shared while we dated and during our marriage.

I talked about how gifted he was in so many areas and how much we loved him and God loved him.

I talked about our son and the great character traits they shared.

We laughed, cried, and, most importantly, we forgave.

As I continued to massage his hands and arms he asked, "Will you pray for me?"

Without hesitation, I placed my hand on his chest and prayed for the Lord to heal him and relieve him of the pain. As the words came out of my mouth, my eyes welled with tears. If I'd had the power to take this away from him, I would have. He closed his eyes and took a deep breath. Then he placed his hands over mine and wouldn't let them go.

When he opened his eyes he said, "Will you marry me?"

And at that, we both laughed! By the end of the visit, he was happy, and so was I.

He died six months later.

———

A good man brings good things out of the good stored up in his heart, and an evil man brings evil things out of the evil stored up in his heart. *For the mouth speaks what the heart is full of.* (Luke 6:45)

Our words reflect what is in our hearts. God had to reveal to me that within my heart was anger toward my husband, pride as a Christian, and self-centeredness in my situation, which is why I was so unhappy. Where was the love? The compassion that reflected his heart?

It wasn't so much the state of my marriage, the challenge with my job situation, or even my overall circumstances in life that was dragging me down. The issue was in how I perceived all the above and what I told myself about them. This was what caused such a roller coaster of negative emotions.

When my words were rooted in the lies of my fickle emotions, they produced a heart of discouragement and disappointment. So God spoke compassion into my life in response to my prayers to help in the transformation of my heart. The Word evoked change. When our hearts and our words line up with those of God, change spills over into our lives.

STEPS TO TALK YOURSELF HAPPY!

How does it all begin? How do we allow God to start transforming our hearts when life happens and it feels as if our world is being turned upside down? We've got to seek God's Word and ask . . .

- *What is in my heart?* This will reveal those areas in our hearts that keep us from true freedom, true joy, and true happiness. Those areas that only the Word of God can penetrate, expose, and heal.
- *What does God want me to learn?* God's ways are opposite of the ways of the world. And if we're honest, our words tend to imitate the world rather than the Word. That's why God often uses life's challenges to help us reevaluate, relearn, and readjust our ways and words so that we can better reflect the heart of God.
- *What are some of God's promises to me?* The power of love, mercy, and forgiveness is a promised gift he gives to us and desires for us to give to others. The act of compassion is a principle we can live by that allows us to be a promise keeper for someone else. After all, heart transformation, word declaration, and the anticipation of God's promise is what we can expect as we talk ourselves happy.

NOW TAKE IT, SPEAK IT, AND LIVE IT!

1. Get together with a friend and recall specific moments the Lord has seen your pain and taken action to help. If he did it before, he'll do it again.

2. Read Psalm 78:38-39 out loud, reminding yourself that God is a God of compassion, *not* condemnation.

3. When you come into conflict with someone, ask God to show you how he sees the other person—with a heart of compassion—and then choose to use your words to heal and empower and not to destroy or tear down. In the end, you'll walk away much more at peace than if you had given in to your initial feelings.

4. Read Ephesians 4:32, Colossians 3:12, and 2 Corinthians 1:3-5, and commit one or more of them to memory, speaking them aloud throughout your day to align your words, your mind, and your heart with the ways, Word, and thoughts of God.

2

trust

You Really Can Trust God!

There has to be some in here somewhere, I thought as I rummaged through every drawer in the kitchen.

"What was I thinking?" I said out loud as I opened the door to an empty pantry. "Faith is one thing, but stupidity is another." I looked around my bare kitchen, wondering if I had lost my mind.

"You did what?" my sister had exclaimed over the phone earlier that week.

"I gave away all my food to the homeless shelter," I told her, rather proud of myself at the time.

"Why?" she asked.

"Well, I believe we're just about to move, so I figured, why not clean house and help the homeless people too?"

She didn't even try to hold back her laughter.

"Don't you think you need to actually have a job before you go giving away all your stuff? Girrrrrl, you better keep that food so you don't go hungry!" she teased.

"God didn't remove me from CBN just to have me sit around here. Of course we're moving, and it's going to happen any day now," I said, attempting to convince myself.

As I leaned against the fridge, my mind wandered back to the year my ex-husband and I had originally bought the house. It was more than seventeen years ago. We had been married six months earlier and were thrilled to purchase our first home together.

"New home, new jobs, new beginning," we had said to each other, giggling like little school kids. God was fulfilling all our dreams, and we were absolutely thrilled to watch everything unfold.

I could see the hand of God quite clearly back then. Everything was so exciting and wonderful: my new job, our marriage, our first home, even the new beach town we were now a part of. We had moved from Columbus, Ohio, to Virginia Beach, Virginia, not too far from the ocean. It had always been a dream of mine to live by the ocean.

My other dream was to work in television. So when I started working for CBN as a television producer for *The 700 Club* and then within the year became a cohost, I was thrilled.

Back then my husband was my best friend, and we loved being in each other's company. We were both big dreamers and driven in our careers. We had so much in common.

Life was so good back then, I thought, completely engrossed in the memory until the sudden noise from the ice maker jolted me back into reality. Then, with a sudden epiphany, I spun around and reached for the handle.

"The freezer! There has to be some in the freezer." Like a

crackhead looking for her next fix, I was on a mad hunt for a piece of chocolate. Chocolate was my *go-to* when I was *going through.* I shoved my arm as far back as I could, forcing my way through bags of frozen peas and a box of expired popsicles.

Jackpot!

There it was. A Ziploc bag with a huge chunk of my son's leftover birthday cake. It was chocolate.

"Praise God!" I ripped open the bag like a wild animal, grabbed a fork, and plopped down in the middle of the family room floor. I didn't care that the cake was harder than a brick. I needed it—now!

Chocolate never failed me.

Chocolate always consoled me.

Chocolate was my great comfort, and I was thankful for it.

I took a huge bite, attempting to ease my anxiety. Pensively, I chewed on the hard cake. On one hand, I was learning lessons about finding joy in the promises of God and looking beyond my own troubles to those of others. But on the other hand, I still had a lot going on in my own life. I was facing some major issues. The number one being finding a job.

I still needed to find a way to support myself and Chase. And it was hard to hold on to faith and not get frustrated. Not only were things not happening the way I had expected, but nothing seemed to be happening *period*! Some days it felt as if God had put my calls on hold, then forgot to get back on the line. His silence was beginning to get the best of me. Still palming the cake like a baseball, I absentmindedly looked out the window. I was confused. And I was disheartened!

"God, you told me to *trust* you, but I have to admit I'm having a difficult time."

As I continued to look out the window my mind kept replaying everything that was still up in the air.

"If I didn't know better, I'd say the more I tell myself to trust you, God, the worse things seem to be," I mumbled.

I thought back to the last day of my job. After fourteen years, I knew it was time to go. A couple of months before I left CBN, the Lord had called me to a forty-day fast during which he spoke to my heart and said, "I'm removing you from this ministry." I was thankful for the hope of working somewhere new.

God's word for me was so special that I jotted down the date in my journal: February 22, 2013. He even confirmed his word through three different ministers on three separate occasions. Each delivered the same promise of what God was preparing to do in my life. A part of me was scared to face change, but for the most part, I was excited about what the future held.

"God sent me here to talk to you," Dr. Myles Munroe had said one day.

I had just finished interviewing him on the set of *The 700 Club* and was joining him and his wife and some of his staff for lunch at a local restaurant.

"God sent me here to prepare you for what is to come," he continued during lunch. "You're going to be called into several meetings back-to-back, and everything is going to shift. It's going to happen faster than you can possibly imagine, but it's all by the hand of God. God is calling you to do something very special. You don't have to worry about how it's going to happen, because God is going to do everything!"

Every word came out slowly and deliberately as he spoke in his Bahamian accent. The presence of the Lord carried such power that everyone who sat at the table fell silent. Then, with an even greater level of intensity, he leaned forward as if to tell me a secret.

"There is a scripture the Lord wants me to share with you, for you to always remember. It's Proverbs 19, verse 21: 'Many are the plans in a person's heart, but it is the LORD's *purpose* that prevails.'"

At the time, I thought I understood that scripture. But it wasn't until I experienced this season of failed plans and unmet expectations that I began to explore what it meant.

Still sitting in the middle of my family room floor, staring out the window as if God was peering back at me, I prayed. "I know what you said, Lord. You said that you would do *everything*, but all I see is *nothing*. You gave me a specific promise, but it looks like the complete opposite is happening! I want to trust you, but I'm struggling with *how* to. I don't understand how you can move me out of one job—not even simply a job, but a major position in a huge ministry—where you promised to do the amazing. . . . But still, nothing? I don't understand. I don't understand how I'm supposed to take care of my son if every door keeps shutting in my face. I feel like you've left me hanging."

I continued, "Lord, I feel like you keep telling me to trust you, but it's as if I'm in a little raft all by myself and the waves of life are just about to flip me over. Lord, I don't understand."

Trust in the Lord with all your heart. Lean not *unto your own understanding. In all your ways acknowledge me, Kristi, and I will direct your paths,* the small voice said.

But the sound of the small voice was steadily being drowned out by my own words of doubt.

By now, the chocolate cake that was meant to bring me comfort was melting in my hand. The whole thing tasted bitter, much like the way I was beginning to feel. Just a year before, when I still had my job and life was rather comfortable, I had sat in this same spot telling the Lord how much I trusted him.

"I'll go wherever you want me to go. I'll do whatever you want me to do," I told the Lord sincerely at the time. But these days I was feeling let down by God, and the constant battle within my soul was poking holes into my faith. My life felt out of control, and I told myself it was time to take back the control I had once signed over to the Lord.

I wanted to be comfortable again.

I wanted to feel secure again.

I wanted to be happy again.

Kristi, go back to the familiar. Go back to the comfortable. Go back to the comfort of coping, and stop chasing hope in the impossible.

The thought of simply focusing on surviving felt safer than continuing to hope in the promise I'd been given, easier than having to face the fear of going forward into a place of the unknown. The scared little girl within me kept saying, *It will be easier to just give up.*

My heart dropped at the weight of my own words. *My words.*

They placed me center ring in the fight for my life. It was a knockout, drag-out fight between the giants of fear and doubt and my faltering belief. And, if truth be told, the giants were winning.

The difficult thing about holding on when we can't see the way forward is that God may reveal what he has in store through the promises he gives to us, but more often than not, he chooses to omit the how, where, or when he's going to fulfill those promises. And the more time passes without us seeing what we're looking for, the more the enemy feeds us a smorgasbord of lying words that create hearts of doubt, fear, and disbelief.

Maybe I heard God wrong, the voice of doubt will whisper.

Maybe I did something that made God change his mind, the voice of fear will say.

Or, *maybe God's promise is actually for someone else,* the voice of disbelief will suggest. Rather than encouraging ourselves with *what we see God do* and *what we know he's done,* we have the tendency to feed our feelings of discouragement by focusing on what we don't see and what we don't know.

Many of us fuel the fires of fear, doubt, and disbelief by talking about people we know who *haven't* received their healing, their financial breakthroughs, restoration of their marriages, or answers to their prayers for families. We choose to see what isn't and choose to speak on what can't and won't be.

As a result, not only do our negative words break down our faith in God, but they also create a breeding ground for discontented lives and discouraged hearts—ultimately making us miserable human beings. And there is nothing worse than being around miserable people. They can suck the happy out of sunshine.

To believe or not to believe. To trust or not to trust. Our words reflect one choice or the other. When we come into agreement with the wrong side, we end up looking at life in the wrong way. And that wrong way leads us to a life that pulls us away from the heart, ways, and Word of God, ultimately limiting the promises he's already spoken over us.

What we must recognize as we fight for our hearts is that it's in the process of the wait that we find the building blocks to our faith. The key to the fulfillment of those promises lies within one word: *trust*.

The gym was a great distraction from my worries. It gave me something to do while I was waiting for God to do something. No one there knew me as the girl on *The 700 Club*. At least, not everybody. Most of them knew me as the girl with the bright pink lipstick who sweated like a pig and grunted while working out. Seeing the same faces every day gave me a sense of connection.

One day as I was finishing up my workout, I ran into an older woman I hadn't seen in weeks. I enjoyed chatting with her, because she was always so upbeat and always had a smile on her face. She was kind of quiet, but her presence was large.

"How have you been?" I asked, stopping to chat on my way out.

"God healed me of cancer!" she proclaimed, the words flying out of her mouth as if waving a flag for the world to see.

"What?" I said, shocked by her bluntness yet thrilled by the news.

IT'S IN THE
PROCESS OF
THE WAIT THAT
WE FIND THE
BUILDING BLOCKS
TO OUR FAITH.

"God healed me of cancer!" she repeated, now drawing the attention of a small group of women who were gathering around her.

"God is so good!" she began as she proceeded to recount the story of her healing. The more she talked, the more her words caused my heart to soar with a rekindled hope for my own life.

"He walked beside me the entire time. He never left me once. In every decision, he was there. At every doctor's appointment he was there. I knew God was going to heal me because he said he would, and he did!" she said as she unabashedly raised her arms in the air and shouted, "Hallelujah!"

There was a fire in this woman's eyes and a power behind her words that inspired me, encouraged me, and slapped me out of my haze of unbelief. She had seen the miraculous power of God firsthand and wanted to tell the world about God's faithfulness. She wasn't just happy; she was elated!

"Every day I get up and praise God for what he's done for me. And I tell him every chance I get, 'Lord, *never* let me forget your goodness in my life.'"

Then, as if she knew my own quiet struggle, she turned to me and said, "Trust him. Regardless of what you see or what you feel, trust him. Whatever he's promised you, he will fulfill, because God is faithful and he loves you, Kristi. He's not a God who lies. God doesn't just tell us that he's trustworthy; he *shows* us that he's trustworthy! So look around you and *see* him. When you get down, tell yourself *who God is*. Then you'll remember what he's done and be encouraged by what he will do!"

Her words pierced my soul so deeply that I couldn't stop

thinking about them the entire drive home. *Who God is . . . who is God?* I mulled, feeling an incredible urge to pick up my Bible and read the passage that answered the question burning within my soul.

> Jesus answered, "*I AM* the way and *the truth* and *the life*. No one comes to the Father except through me." (John 14:6)

Although I had known this passage since childhood, God did something really cool that afternoon as he brought new meaning to his Word through the Holy Spirit. Here is what he illuminated for me:

- **I am the way.** God's Word will lead us and guide us in the way we should go. God's promises are not hidden from us. When we seek him in prayer and in his Word, guided by the power of the Holy Spirit, he will lead us right into those promises. When we feel lost or discouraged, we've got to remind ourselves that God is trustworthy.
- **I am the truth.** God's Word is the truth. It's the only thing that counteracts and beats down the lies of the enemy that threaten to drive our minds, mouths, and hearts down into the pit. So we must speak the truth of God's Word to blast out the roadblocks of discouragement, fear, and doubt. Speaking the truth is how we can talk our way back on track, aiming toward the promise land.

- **I am the life.** It's the power of the Holy Spirit that
  breathes life and goodness into our situations. As we
  speak the Word of God, we are speaking life into our
  situations, life into our hearts, and life that infuses
  hope for what's to come. Our words of life will not only
  encourage us in the journey, but just like the testimony
  of the older woman encouraged me and fueled my faith,
  we must allow our spoken testimony to encourage others
  and fuel their faith. God promises us life, and not just
  life, but life more abundant! In times of trouble, we've got
  to tell ourselves that.

Jesus continues to talk to his disciples about the hope of
what is to come in regard to preparing a place for his followers
in heaven with his Father. As Jesus talked, one of the disciples
asked to see the Father. Jesus responded,

"If you really know me, you will know my Father as well.
From now on, *you do know him and have* seen *him.*"
    Philip said, "Lord, show us the Father and *that will
be enough for us.*"
    Jesus answered: *"Don't you know me,* Philip, even
after I have been among you such a long time? . . .
    Don't you believe that I am in the Father, and that
the Father is in me? . . .
    Believe me when I say that I am in the Father and
the Father is in me; or *at least believe on the evidence of
the works themselves.* (John 14:7–11)

Philip did what we all do. He questioned or, some might say even doubted, the very thing that Jesus had already promised him—in this case, the promise to see God the Father. But Philip, like many of us, couldn't recognize what was right in front of him. At times we all get so focused on what we see or what we understand that we neglect to embrace the greatness of the unseen and the not understood. But that's the essence of faith!

Hebrews 11:1 tells us, "Now faith is the substance of things hoped for, the evidence of things *not seen*" (NKJV).

Faith works completely differently than the physical world. The physical world says, "I've got to see it to believe it." The faith world says, "I've got to believe it to see it." Faith works in the realm of belief, trust, and knowing: belief that God's Word is true, trust that God is who he says he is, and knowing that God is a God who doesn't lie.

What both reflects and fuels our faith? The words we speak. Because what we speak reveals what we believe and then turns around and builds up that belief even more. The key to faith in times when things seem unclear is to believe in the unseen—and make sure your words reflect that belief—so that you can actually see. It sounds crazy, but it's true.

The Lord knows that we all struggle with faith in him at times and that it's a constant battle within us to want to *see* God move a bit more clearly and definitely a lot sooner than he often does. And yet God rarely fulfills his promises when we want him to or in the way we expect. He fulfills them according to his plan, which is ultimately for our good. I love that along the way, the

AT TIMES WE ALL GET
SO FOCUSED ON WHAT
WE SEE OR WHAT WE
UNDERSTAND THAT WE
NEGLECT TO EMBRACE
THE GREATNESS OF
THE UNSEEN AND THE
NOT UNDERSTOOD.

Lord continually encourages us by *showing* himself through his works. We just have to see it.

The second part of John 14:11 reveals this element of God's graciousness toward his children. Knowing our struggles, he helps us to see the evidence of his faithfulness in our lives so that we can be encouraged to face our current challenges and trust him with them.

> Believe me when I say that I am in the Father and the Father is in me; or *at least believe on the evidence of the works themselves.* (NKJV)

Believe on the evidence of the works themselves. God shows us in countless ways that he's trustworthy by the evidence of his handprint on our lives. The question we must ask ourselves is, what do we see God doing?

What evidence do we have that God is working on our behalf?

And what evidence do we have that God is blessing us, helping us, loving us, providing for us, and guiding us toward the goodness of his promises for us? We have to tell ourselves the ways that we see him.

When I reread John 14 after getting home from the gym, I imagined my own version of the conversation between Jesus and his disciples. But this time, I brought the story into modern day and imagined that Jesus was talking to us, his followers. I could hear the frustration in Jesus' voice as he tried to convince us that the thing we're looking for is the very thing that is right in front of us.

"Do you see me?" I imagined Jesus asking. "Do you see the evidence of my works?"

I heard—as his words brought forth life, speaking hope, truth, and faith back into the atmosphere, breaking through the clouds of discouragement—"You've seen me heal the sick. You've seen me deliver the oppressed. You've even seen me feed the hungry. So tell me, tell others, but, most important, tell *yourself* what you see."

Then I imagined the conversation shifting, and Jesus turning to me and asking,

"Kristi, you're worried about a job, but aren't *all* your bills paid? *Do you see me?*"

"Kristi, you're worried about taking care of your son, but is he lacking in any area of his life? *Do you see me?*"

"Kristi, you're fretting over not having a husband to help you, but have I protected you, provided for you, and loved you? *Do you see me?*"

"Kristi, you're so focused on the hope in the future that you've neglected to see the happy in the now. *Do you see me?*"

Trust. We can get so sidetracked by our own perspectives of how things should be that when life doesn't turn out exactly that way, we lose sight of what God is doing, how he's fulfilling his promises to us. And so we end up unhappy. But we don't have to stay in that place.

One way to talk ourselves happy is to readjust our conversations by not talking about the failures of man and instead talking about the faithfulness of God. If God said it, he's going to do it, but we need to ask ourselves honestly if God said it in the first place. I can't tell you how many times I set my mind on something, begged God to make it happen, and then ended up wallowing in a cloud of disappointment because what I expected didn't happen.

As believers, sometimes we get into the habit of placing expectations on God that he never agreed to. Then when we don't get what we want, we blame him, telling ourselves that God let us down. When we feed that mind-set by speaking that lie to ourselves and to others, it's as if we are creating a strike against God's trustworthiness. That's why we need the Word of God to counteract the lies of the enemy and the lies we tell ourselves. We must pursue the truth, because the truth not only sets us free, it ushers us into a place of happiness.

The true essence of trust is the ability to cast aside our own understanding of a situation and have the courage to surrender to the only One who fully knows all aspects of the situation. Trust relinquishes control and relies on someone or something other than ourselves.

For instance, when we get on an airplane, we trust that a four-hundred-plus-ton piece of metal is going to soar miles up into the sky to take us where we need to go.

We trust that it's going to keep us in the air.

We trust that we're going to be safe in the process.

And we trust that we're going to get to our destination on time. Yet many of us have more faith in a giant piece of metal than we do in the One who created the metal.

Think about it. Why do we trust planes? It seems to make no logical sense. But we do it anyway. First, many of us trust planes because of the *general* knowledge that planes are reliable and safe. Second, and perhaps more convincingly, many of us trust planes because of our *personal* experience of flying and then determining that planes are reliable and safe. Even though we can recall a handful of times when planes have failed to meet our expectations, overall we choose to place our trust in them and continue to fly.

It's the same with our relationship with God. We may know generally that he is trustworthy, but it's even more powerful when we know personally from our experience that he is faithful. Then, even in those few times when we feel that God has let us down, which could be due to our own flawed perceptions, we can remember the number of other times he has proved himself to be reliable, good, safe, and trustworthy.

How do we go from a general knowledge of God to a personal experience with him? It starts by learning about, or in some cases reminding ourselves of, who God is and connecting with his heart, his character, and his ways. When we plant these truths deep in our hearts, our eyes start to open and we begin to see, perhaps in ways we hadn't noticed before, the little ways God has demonstrated these truths to us personally.

Let's get practical and look at how we can talk ourselves happy. The answer is found when we tell ourselves *how* God is, *who* God is, and *what* God says.

How God Is

- God is faithful.
- God is true.
- God is alive.
- God is honest.
- God is for us not against us.
- God is loyal.
- God is active.
- God is present.
- God is mindful.
- God is personal.
- God is an anchor.
- God is love.

Who God Is

- God is all powerful.
- God is all encompassing.
- God is all sufficient.
- God is all knowing.
- God is all right.
- And, as my mom says, "God will not allow us to be overtaken by the challenges of life!"

What God Says

- God will never lie to us. (Numbers 23:19)
- God will never abandon us. (Deuteronomy 31:8)
- God will always be loyal to us. (Deuteronomy 31:8)

- God loves us unconditionally. (Romans 8:35; 1 John 4:7, 8)
- God will never fail to fulfill his promises to us. (Deuteronomy 31:8)
- God will never give up on us. (Hebrews 13:5)
- God will never get tired of being there for us. (Isaiah 40:28)
- God will protect us. (Psalm 18:30)
- God will keep us safe when we trust him. (Proverbs 2:1–11)
- God will direct us. (Proverbs 3:5–6)
- God will not hold a grudge against us. (Daniel 9:9)
- God will always forgive us. (Psalm 103:12)
- God will always provide for us. (Matthew 6:28–33)
- God will give us good gifts because he is good. (James 1:17)
- God can do anything for us. (Matthew 19:26)

God shows himself to us. Not only through his Word, but through the evidence of his Word that is alive, active, and unmistakably present in our lives. Every time he shows us that he's trustworthy, we need to encourage ourselves with that evidence by talking about it! Just as the woman at the gym did.

The power of her words jump-started the faith of every woman in that small circle listening to her. She reminded us that God has our back. And he loves us unconditionally, even during those times when we struggle with doubt, fear, and disbelief.

It is so wonderful that to know God is to know the hope we have in him. Hope that reminds us that if he said it, he will do it—and that's enough to talk yourself happy!

Whoever trusts in the LORD, happy is he. (Proverbs 16:20 NKJV)

STEPS TO TALK YOURSELF HAPPY

We live in a world where everything is determined by what we see. But our goal is to see in a different way. It's all about acknowledging the handprint of God on our lives and encouraging ourselves in the knowing that God is actively working on our behalf! Here are some baseline questions to ask as you seek to develop a heart transformed by trust.

- *What are some of the things God has done in your life that confirm who God is to you?* No matter how small or seemingly insignificant, use those moments to encourage yourself in the difficult seasons when your faith takes a nose dive.
- *When you feel defeated, how do you respond?* Sometimes when we get discouraged we pull away from the things of God. We stop going to church. We stop reading his Word. And we stop hanging out with believers who have the power to fuel our faith. Get back in the game, and get back in the Word. Reacquaint yourself with the love of God while asking him to reignite your faith in him.

NOW TAKE IT, SPEAK IT, AND LIVE IT!

1. Make a conscious effort to silence the lies of the enemy about God's trustworthiness with the truth of what you know about God.

2. Go to one of your partners in Christ and ask that person to keep you accountable for your words: the words you're speaking and also whose words you are believing.

3. Get together with your friends and share your stories about what God has done for you. It will fuel your faith and reignite your hope in God.

identity

This Is Who You Really Are

I was trying to skip out of church early so that no one would notice me as folks filed out of the service. That had become my M.O.

I'm not sure when it began, but somewhere along the way I had become super self-conscious and overly insecure about everything. I was convinced people could see all my failures and shortcomings by merely peering into my eyes. The fear of exposing the truth of what my life was really like these days created a concoction of anxiety and worry that stirred within my soul, hijacking any semblance of peace.

What I did for a living had come to define me, and now, without the big titles and fancy labels, I wasn't so sure who I was anymore. I felt lost.

"What are you doing these days?"

"Where are you working now?"

"You're still not married yet?"

In my mind those questions roughly translated to "What's

wrong with you?" and "Do you realize there must be something wrong with you?"

When people asked me these questions, it always set off a ringing in my ears and increased my heartbeat so much that I was sure it was visible through my shirt. My forced smile concealed the instant sensation of cotton mouth at their inquisition. I just wanted them all to shut up and leave me alone.

Somewhere down the line I got it into my mind that the world was judging me because I didn't measure up to its standards. The same standards that I so readily agreed to and strived to meet. The standards that society defined as "the image of success." Success, nonetheless, that was based upon a false sense of perfection. I spent years and years in pursuit of the perfect body.

The perfect career.

The perfect house.

The perfect spouse.

The perfect kids.

And the perfect dream of wholeness and happiness that came in the promise of all the above.

I was coming to the realization that there was a deficit within my soul, however, and a new job, a new husband, and a new life would not fill it up and make me happy. Yes, there had been plenty of moments when these things had brought me a sense of happiness, joy even. But the problem was that because those things I pursued were temporary, so, too, was my happiness—forever fleeting.

I felt the way my son usually did a week after Christmas. Having discovered under the tree Christmas morning that one special thing he had begged for and could not live without, he would be so happy he could barely contain himself. Fast forward a week or two later, though, and that very thing that brought him to a place of euphoria was now thrown in the corner with last year's "I can't live without it" thing.

I was no different.

"Jesus, if you just give me this amazing job, then I'll be happy."

"Jesus, if you just help me lose this weight, then I'll be happy."

"Jesus, if you just bring me that tall, hot, crazy gorgeous, rich husband, then I'll be happy."

But I wasn't happy, even when God blessed me with those things. The pursuit of *things* rather than the pursuit of the One who blessed me with those *things* often left me with a bad after-taste. Kind of the way artificial flavoring does. Those *things* disappointed me, leaving me wanting more. But my pursuit of more only left me with a case of the "not enough."

Just love your husband *more*—but it wasn't enough because he left anyway.

Just work *more* hours to climb the corporate ladder—but it wasn't enough because I was booted out anyway.

Just exercise *more* to get that perfect body—but that wasn't enough because that one extra chocolate chip cookie blew up my thighs to look like an inflatable inner tube anyway.

More was never enough.

Speed walking to my car, I unconsciously ran my hand over my hair in an attempt to stuff the unruly pieces back into my thinning ponytail. "Stop fidgeting," the floor director would

MY PURSUIT
OF MORE ONLY
LEFT ME WITH
A CASE OF THE
"NOT ENOUGH."

always tell me on the set of *The 700 Club.* I couldn't help it. It was something I did when I was anxious.

"Are you excited?" I heard a voice behind me yell, clearly attempting to get my attention.

"Your birthday! It's coming up in a couple of weeks, right?!" My friend was trotting in her heels to catch up with me as I was hurrying to get into my car.

"Wanna do something to celebrate?" she asked enthusiastically while trying to catch her breath.

"No, not really," I said, trying to mask any sign that my heart was dropping at the very mention of my upcoming birthday. "I mean, it's just another day, no big deal," I responded with a half smile.

As I turned the key to unlock my car door I stared over at my son, widening my eyes a bit so he could catch my signal—the signal that nine times out of ten he missed. So I tried the ventriloquist routine to reinforce the message by mumbling, "Hurry up and get in the car."

I was turning forty-four years old. Middle-aged, according to my twelve-year-old son. "I'm not middle-aged. I'm still young and hot, right?" I had teased him a couple of weeks ago as he watched me place a batch of brownies into the oven.

Not amused, he'd looked meaningfully at me as I stood in the kitchen with my oversized sweat pants and a T-shirt exhibiting a wonderful array of splatters and drips from the brownie mix I was licking off the big mixing spoon.

When was the last time I washed that shirt? I thought as I pulled out of the church parking lot.

Forty-four, I repeated in my head. This was not what the forties are supposed to look like. Your forties are when you finally get into the groove of life, when you feel more settled and more stable in all your roles. You know who you are and why you're here, right? *But nothing could be farther from the truth*, I thought, as I drove down the winding road toward my house.

Here I was, a forty-something-year-old unemployed, divorced–widowed single mom fighting the battle of the bulge and living off her son's college savings. I had no clue who I was anymore and was struggling to make sense of it all. In fact, any day now I was expecting someone to ring my doorbell and shout, "Smile! You're on *Candid Camera.*"

Still, I had committed to trusting God in this process of my life; I was just trying to figure out what that really meant. My days were spent studying the Bible and crying out to God, but rather than feeling all warm and fuzzy, I was feeling like my life was in the eye of the storm.

The house of cards I had meticulously built over the years was falling apart before my very eyes. The things that had seemed to anchor me were either gone or morphing into something unfamiliar. From my career to my financial status, from my relationships to my physical, mental, and emotional states, I felt powerless.

I felt vulnerable.

I felt unstable.

I was lost.

"What is going on, Lord? I need help," I said, as I drove into my driveway, passing the "For Sale" sign on my front lawn.

"I have enough equity in my house to just sell it and buy a small townhouse or condo," I'd said to my parents.

Unable to get a job for almost two years had put me under financial strain. We lived in an amazing house in a great neighborhood, and money or the lack thereof was a definite factor in choosing to put my house on the market after living there for more than seventeen years. I wasn't sure if I was doing the right thing, but I had to do something. Another card in my perfect world falling down.

I just needed help.

Help in knowing what to do and where to go.

Help in deciphering the truth of God's Word and how it played out in my life.

And, most of all, help in keeping my sanity and peace as opposed to the worry and anxiety I felt every day.

The next morning I stood in front of my bathroom mirror consumed by the image staring back at me. It wasn't the kind of "Girl, you are working it!" moment as much as a "Girl, you look a hot mess and need to get yourself together!" moment. You know when you see those before and after pictures in the magazines and are amazed by how good the after picture looks? Well, my life was kind of like that, only the reverse.

My normally long, perfectly styled hair was neglected and unkempt. I couldn't afford to go to the hairdresser, so between my home remedies and the premenopausal-stressed-out-sweat-like-a-maniac incidents, my hair was breaking off in clumps. Also, this season of worry and anxiety had turned me into a full-fledged chocoholic, so my usually semi-fit physique was transforming into some foreign specimen I did not recognize. The "Ms. America look" that was once a mandate before walking out of the house was now a thing of the past.

"Mom, my hair is falling out! My stomach feels like I might have an ulcer. Oh, and I still can't get a job!" I whined to my mother over the phone. I was anticipating, even goading her into some sort of consoling remark that would soothe my "woe is me" moment. But instead of sympathy she responded as if she were watching a stand-up bit on Comedy Central.

Here I was, sharing all the heartbreak moments that make up the perfect lyrics to a blues song, and this woman could not stop laughing! Although I tried to act insulted by her insensitive response, her laughter evoked a reactionary bout of laughter within me. Before long we were both in tears.

Classic.

Once we finally composed ourselves enough to hear each other speak, she said, "Girl, you went from a peacock to a feather duster."

The word picture was like a bucket of ice-cold water being poured down my back. She was right on. As I pictured a peacock I immediately thought of its grand appearance and the value that was assigned by its spectacular presentation to the world.

The praise and accolades that drove it to puff its feathers out while strutting its stuff, showcasing its awesomeness for the world to see.

Its unique color palette of feathers bouncing in the wind, beckoning onlookers to "Look at me. Look at me. I'm important. I'm valuable. I am somebody."

I was embarrassed to realize how uncomfortably familiar this was to my own life. Well, my old life. Even as a Christian I gauged my success, worth, and happiness on what I had, who others thought I was, and how I felt about myself. The pursuit of the "I" was destroying my life, and just as the quest to obtain a life of perfection was a fruitless endeavor, so, too, seemed my hope for a life filled with long-lasting peace, joy, and happiness.

> Do not be *conformed* to this world, but be *transformed* by the *renewal of your mind*, that by testing you may discern what is the *will of God*, what is good and acceptable and perfect. (Romans 12:2 ESV)

Sometimes—a lot of the time—when we feel that our problems are insurmountable and we are lost in the midst of them, we spend days and nights begging God to change our circumstances when the truth is, what really needs changing is *us*. Point blank. Period.

How we think, what we believe, and what we say are all reflections of who we think we are, of what's really in our hearts. When we look at what's coming out of our mouths in our conversations with loved ones and even in our talks with God, what do we see? Do our words reflect an out-of-balance focus on what we perceive to be the ideal plans for our lives—in other words, our plans—or an unhealthy obsession with our worldly status, or maybe too much value placed on what our friends think of us?

Usually, what comes to light is that the root of our problems has very little to do with things like the job market or our relationship status. It's us. God needs to hit the reset button on our beings and restore our focus from our current positions in life to the purpose he has for our lives! But our purpose can't be fulfilled or even defined until his *new* for us is established. The new that will unfold as we allow God to give us a new mind—his mind.

A new heart—his heart.

And a new image—his image.

Ephesians 4:24 tells us to "Put on the new self, created to be like God in true righteousness and holiness." But the process of removing or taking something off that has been a part of you for longer than you can imagine is not an easy task. And I'm not just talking difficult. I'm talking painful! You know, the kind of pain that feels like someone is slowly ripping duct tape from the most delicate part of your skin. That kind of pain.

It's amazing how comfortable we can become with ourselves. Even justifying our attitudes and behaviors when someone challenges us to change. If something we say rubs someone the wrong way, we tend to justify ourselves with excuses like, "That's just my personality. This is how I am." But if your "I am" is not like the Great I Am, then somebody's got to change, and it's not him.

A while back, I was invited to speak at a women's conference. Ironically, the theme of the conference was "Be Brave, Be True, Be You." When I first heard the theme I thought it sounded like a bumper sticker, but I was ready to roll with it. About a month before the conference, I set off to prepare by collecting verses on the topic. But something was different this time. The process was like walking through quicksand while having shackles clasped to my ankles. I wasn't getting anywhere.

"Lord, what in the world is going on? Help me get this

IF YOUR "I AM" IS NOT LIKE THE GREAT I AM, THEN SOMEBODY'S GOT TO CHANGE, AND IT'S NOT HIM.

done," I pleaded week after week as the conference date drew nearer.

Day after day, I painstakingly sifted through scriptures like "We are made in the image of Christ" (Genesis 1:26), "We are fearfully and wonderfully made" (Psalm 139:14), and "We are the head and not the tail, above and not beneath" (Deuteronomy 28:13). I wrote pages and pages of talking points, each ending up in the wastebasket. "Help me, Lord!" I cried with a sense of desperation.

Then, as if the verbal declaration alone would snap me into a place of clarity and healing, I shouted, "*I am* made in the image of Christ. *I am* the head and not the tail. *I am* above and not beneath." Allowing the words to linger in the air, anticipating some immediate revelatory change within, I continued to sit there. Nothing. Diverting my attention to the Bible and staring intently at the verses of Scripture I had just recited, I questioned, "What do these words even mean?"

I was reading all the right scriptures—even attempting to speak those same verses over my life—but for some reason, the words that I spoke fell flat. They felt like mere words without meaning or revelation. Something was clearly missing. There was a disconnect somewhere within me that didn't allow the words to penetrate my heart and override the already established thoughts in my mind.

Laying the Bible down on the couch I walked over to the window and stared at the leaves that were beginning to change colors.

I prayed: "What's wrong with me, Lord? I'm doing everything I know to do. Yet I feel like I'm just banging my head against the wall. At times, Lord, I feel like I move two steps forward in my relationship with you. Then other times I feel like I take ten steps backward, fighting the same stupid fight within my mind all over again. Jesus, you're all I have, and I need you! I need your help with this conference. I need your help with my life. I need your help with, well, me!"

It was a long while before I spoke again. Then, like a whisper spoken into the depth of my soul, I heard the Lord. "You read the Word, Kristi, but you don't always *believe* the Word."

Believe: "To accept something as true. To feel sure of the truth. To expect or hope with confidence; to trust." *(Merriam-Webster Dictionary)*

It is so easy for us to believe what the Word of God says for someone else but not so easy when it comes to ourselves. It's not that we doubt God's Word, but sometimes how we feel about ourselves affects our belief. For instance, we can take a scripture that says something like, "I am fearfully and wonderfully made" (Psalm 139:14), and disagree with the Word by asking ourselves "If I'm so 'fearfully and wonderfully made,' then why am I such a failure in certain areas of my life?"

The battle in our minds is real. When we nurture negative and false ideas about our lives, solidified by the words we speak to ourselves and others, then often our attempts to embrace the truth of who we are based upon the Word of God can prove extremely difficult. At times, impossible.

When we realize we're allowing negative thoughts to shape how we see ourselves and the world around us, then it's time to make a change. It's important to discover not only how to speak right, but how to think right. And how to believe right. After all, belief is the link that ties trust and faith together. It's impossible to have one without the other, because one *is* the other.

How can we get our words, thoughts, and beliefs about ourselves and how God sees us to line up with the Word of God? And how can we believe the words we tell ourselves and shore up our faith so that it doesn't crash and burn so frequently?

Jesus alone carries the power to transform what we see, think, speak, and believe about who we are. When we cry out to Jesus with sincere hearts, he never fails to graciously lift us up with his loving hand.

We can begin the process of revelation and transformation by talking to God and asking Jesus:

- How do I allow your Word to change how I *feel* about myself?
- How do I allow your Word to change how I *think* about myself?
- And how do I see your Word as more than just words on a page, but words that impact and empower as I *speak* them to myself?

Words come by way of three different sources: God, the enemy, and ourselves. We know that every word that comes out of the mouth of God is true (Numbers 23:19). And every word that comes out of the mouth of the enemy is a lie (John 8:44). And when it comes to us, well, many of us take on an either-or approach depending on which way the wind is blowing. The question we must ask is, *whose* word are we choosing to believe?

Words are power no matter where they originate. They have a huge impact on our perspective. And that perspective can either help our faith grow and increase, or our perspective on things can stunt or even sabotage our faith. We need to plug into the one true source of power, allowing the words we read, hear, and speak to fuel our faith, igniting change within our lives.

Back to my original question: How? How do we allow the Word of God to rise up off the physical pages of the Bible and plant itself into the recesses of our minds, transforming our old thoughts, attitudes, and issues of the heart?

There is a lamp in the corner of my office that I think of when I consider this question.

Not too long ago, I tried to turn it on, but it didn't work. I flipped the switch on and off a couple of times, but nothing. I changed the lightbulb. Nothing. I spun the lamp around, readjusted the bulb again, and, still, nothing. I was dumbfounded.

Then Chase got up from playing one of his video games, walked over to the lamp, picked up the cord, and plugged it into the wall outlet. He flipped the switch, and the light came on. Then, without speaking a single word, he turned around, walked back to his seat, and continued to play his game.

All that confusion, and I had forgotten to plug the stupid thing in.

A lamp is just a piece of furniture until it's plugged into a power source. When light emanates from that lamp it brings forth more than light. It brings forth clarity, even life, into the room. In the same way, the words written on the pages of the Bible can feel like mere words until they are empowered by the Holy Spirit, making the Word alive. It's the Holy Spirit who transforms mere words and touches something inside of us, miraculously conforming our minds into the mind of Christ and revamping our hearts to reflect the heart of God!

We often neglect to recognize the presence of the Holy Spirit as the link that takes us from the old person to the new, but we need to remember that the indwelling of the Holy Spirit (Romans 8:9) reproduces the life of Jesus in our own lives! That's why he's an integral part of our Christian walk. When we continually depend on the Holy Spirit for guidance, power, and direction, we will see the old ways of thinking, believing, and living transform into the new ways promised in Christ.

What does this look like? How does the Holy Spirit reveal himself as that ever-present help (Psalm 46:1)? Below are just a few of the ways the Holy Spirit works in our lives.

- The Holy Spirit *helps* us:

   "But the *Helper*, the Holy Spirit, whom the Father will send in my name, he will teach you all things and bring to your remembrance all that I have said to you" (John 14:26 ESV).
- The Holy Spirit *intercedes* for us:

   "Likewise the Spirit helps us in our weakness. For we do not know what to pray for as we ought, but the Spirit himself *intercedes* for us with groanings too deep for words" (Romans 8:26 ESV).

- The Holy Spirit gives us *truth*:

    "When the Spirit of truth comes, he will *guide you into all the truth*, for he will not speak on his own authority, but whatever he hears he will speak, and he will declare to you the things that are to come" (John 16:13 ESV).

- The Holy Spirit gives us *understanding, wisdom, counsel, and strength*:

    "And the Spirit of the LORD shall rest upon him, the Spirit of *wisdom* and *understanding*, the Spirit of *counsel* and *might*, the Spirit of *knowledge* and the fear of the LORD" (Isaiah 11:2 ESV).

- The Holy Spirit gives us *boldness* in our words:

    "And when they had prayed, the place in which they were gathered together was shaken, and they were all filled with the Holy Spirit and continued to speak the word of God with *boldness*" (Acts 4:31 ESV).

- The Holy Spirit gives us *joy, peace, kindness,* and *goodness*:

    "But the fruit of the Spirit is love, *joy, peace,* patience, *kindness, goodness,* faithfulness, gentleness, self-control; against such things there is no law" (Galatians 5:22–23 ESV).

- The Holy Spirit gives us *freedom*:

    "Now the Lord is the Spirit, and where the Spirit of the Lord is, there is *freedom*" (2 Corinthians 3:17 ESV).

- The Holy Spirit gives us *hope*:

    "May the God of *hope* fill you with all *joy and peace in believing*, so that by the power of the Holy Spirit you may abound in hope" (Romans 15:13 ESV).

Having a better understanding of the role of the Holy Spirit in our lives, we can ask him to help us put on the new self by changing the way we speak and the way we pray. In my case, I'm trying to put into practice the habit of no longer arguing with or rejecting what God has spoken about who I am. When I read a passage in the Bible such as "I am fearfully and wonderfully made," I will choose to receive that truth, accept his Word into my heart and my mind, and then let my words reflect it.

It's about allowing our spoken words to affirm his living Word. We have to make a conscious choice to speak only words that agree with what God says about us. And if ever we find ourselves going down a slippery slope by speaking negative or untruthful or damaging words, then we've got to quickly ask God to forgive us and immediately get back on course with who he says we are, not who the enemy or the world or even we ourselves say we are.

Happiness is knowing that in God we are free from all the misguided standards placed on us by a broken society. We are his children, and we are made in his image. We have to remind ourselves that every wonderful characteristic found in God is also in us when we are in him. So let's hold on to that by speaking it in and over our lives—and get happy about it!

It was the morning of the women's conference, and the Lord woke me up at 5:30. For the past couple of weeks I had made the choice to surrender my life to the things of God and allow the Holy Spirit to guide me in "spirit and in truth" (John 4:24).

HAPPINESS IS
KNOWING THAT
IN GOD WE ARE
FREE FROM ALL
THE MISGUIDED
STANDARDS
PLACED ON US BY A
BROKEN SOCIETY.

Teaching me who I was in him. I had settled my heart to cast all my cares on the Lord each day, refusing to worry about the stupid things I always seemed to worry about.

I was no longer afraid of getting in front of a group of women who might judge me as they inspected me. I didn't care in the least bit. Seriously. I can't explain how or when it happened, but clearly the power of the Holy Spirit pushed out all those nagging areas of insecurities and doubt. He redirected my focus more so on him than on anything else.

Speak the truth, Kristi. Get up on stage, and tell the women the truth, I heard the Lord say to my heart early that morning. I had an immediate understanding of what God was asking me to do. Having worked in media for more than twenty years, I was a part of the propaganda machine that got people to buy into the false illusion of perfection. The hope in a perfect-looking life that promised eternal happiness.

It was all a farce.

That morning I dressed completely differently than the way the old Kristi used to dress. It's not that there was anything wrong with how I used to dress—you know, the "TV look" with the perfect hair, makeup, outfit, and killer shoes. It's just that God was doing a new thing in me, and it wasn't necessary for my looks to overshadow what he was doing in my heart. After all, it wasn't about me, but rather what the Lord wanted to do through me! So, instead of the fancy dress I had planned to wear, I opted for a pair of comfortable black jeans, a cute jacket, and some sneakers.

"God, it's all good. Do what you want to do today, and help *me* not get in the way of *you*."

When I got on stage, I poured my heart out to the women. I talked about what the Lord had done and was still doing in my life. I talked about every insecurity and flaw, and I even talked about my many areas of regret—such as the years I had walked in self-righteousness rather than humility, hard-heartedness rather than compassion, and anger rather than forgiveness.

But most important, I talked about the power of God and how in spite of our issues, mishaps, mistakes, and misguided images of ourselves, the power of God will never fail to transform us if we just let him. The key to change lies within each of us: Jesus Christ resides inside of us *to empower us*!

The wisdom of the words I spoke that day didn't come from me but from the Holy Spirit within me. When I stepped aside and made room for the Holy Spirit to move within the hearts of the women there, God did just that.

He moved.

He healed.

He loved.

He consoled.

He renewed.

And he redefined.

When the conference was over and I was back at home, I passed by the mirror I had wasted countless hours standing in front of, the mirror that had highlighted every flaw and imperfection. But this time my mind was so overwhelmed by what God had done for all of us women at the conference that I didn't give the image in the mirror a second thought. What happened that afternoon was a miracle. God used my words, his words, to bring life. And what was so cool was that the conference title "Be Brave, Be True, Be You" no longer sounded like a bumper sticker but instead became our motto.

- **Brave**—allowing the Holy Spirit to give us the courage to face the lies of what we've been telling ourselves
- **True**—allowing the Holy Spirit to help us embrace the truth of who God says we are by the Word of the only One who represents the truth
- **You**—allowing the Holy Spirit to reveal who *you* represent, who *you* stand for, and who *you* are made in the image of. That is Jesus Christ. And it's by leaning into the power of the Holy Spirit as he reveals the things of Jesus Christ that we experience true happiness and a joy complete.

STEPS TO TALK YOURSELF HAPPY

Every day we are bombarded with messages that try to define who we are, but God's view of us is all that matters. When we choose to see ourselves as God sees us while receiving from him all that he desires to give us, that's when our lives will be transformed and our joy will be fulfilled. Here are a few questions to think about as you walk this road.

- *How do you generally feel, think, and speak about yourself, and do they align with God's Word?* It's time to ask God to reveal the areas within your heart that need some fine-tuning and maybe a good dose of truth. Remember, happiness comes from within, so allow God to work from the inside out.

- *What are you putting more work into: the reflection in the mirror or the reflection of your heart?* While God can change our circumstances in the blink of an eye, he is more concerned about changing our hearts in the midst of our circumstances. So, let him do his thing.

NOW TAKE IT, SPEAK IT, AND LIVE IT!

1. Get together with a friend to pray and ask God for help truly believing his Word and seeing yourselves as he sees you. Check in with each other during the course of the next week and continue praying together.
2. Remind yourself of the role of the Holy Spirit in your life, and consciously address this person of the Trinity in your prayers, seeking his power to lead you into the truth of God's Word for your life.
3. Read what the Bible says about who we are in Christ, and commit one or two verses to memory. Here are just a few suggestions: John 1:12, Romans 6:6, 1 Peter 2:9, and Colossians 3:1.

4

obedience

Love Will Set You Free

I knew it was wrong. Everything in me knew it was wrong, but I justified it. Minimized it, even tried to convince myself by saying, "I deserve it. It's not that big a deal. Besides, God loves me and wants me to be happy. It makes me happy."

The truth was that it filled a need within me that I told myself God was not filling. I did what I wanted to do in spite of knowing that it went against the heart and ways of God.

"It slow-walks you down," my mother warned me. "It may seem small and insignificant, but every act of disobedience against the Word of God comes with a price tag, Kristi. Some price tags are heftier than others, but there is always a price to be paid and a consequence to face."

"But Jesus paid the price for our sins. So, God will forgive me," I said.

"Yes, he did. And yes, he will. But willful disobedience against the heart of God—when we know what's right yet deliberately choose to do what's wrong—will hinder all the wonderful things God desires to bless us with. God established guidelines for us as a way to help and protect us. Because he loves us."

Why was it so difficult to do what was right versus what *felt* right? God's standard was crystal clear, but it was as if I was trying to rewrite God's Word to accommodate my own selfish desires. I started looking the other way, as if to somehow proclaim my sin as okay, as right even, despite the fact that God had declared it wrong.

This particular battle had started because I told myself God was taking too long. I had grown tired of waiting for him to give me what I wanted . . . what he promised me. But just as my mother said, it was slow-walking me down. Every bit of happiness and enjoyment I initially felt was replaced by the guilt, shame, and regret that was leaving me worse than before.

It was suffocating me.

"God, you haven't. God, you didn't. God, when will you?" are the words the enemy plays back to us when he dangles his counter-feit before our eyes, promising to give us what we tell ourselves God is withholding from us. If we're not careful, feelings of hopelessness and weariness in the wait become fertile ground for the seed of temptation to take root and grow by the watering of our words.

We don't realize that before any act of disobedience is con-ceived, often we have already given it power. We have allowed a simple thought to mull around in our minds, birthing in us a belief that God has failed us. We tell ourselves, therefore, that the only way to get what we want is to take matters into our own hands. We talk ourselves miserable by talking ourselves into sin: the sin of placing self over the sacrifices of God.

IF WE'RE NOT
CAREFUL, FEELINGS
OF HOPELESSNESS
AND WEARINESS IN THE
WAIT BECOME FERTILE
GROUND FOR THE SEED
OF TEMPTATION TO
TAKE ROOT AND GROW
BY THE WATERING OF
OUR WORDS.

We set the sin into motion with our words when we murmur or complain about our circumstances, which eventually leads to us grabbing hold of Satan's counterfeit rather than grabbing hold of the truth of God's Word. Why does this inevitably happen? Because every time we speak against what God has spoken to us, we negate the same promises we're waiting for God to fulfill.

Sin is a thief, and disobedience is its accomplice. The sin birthed from our continual disobedience will steal everything that God has blessed us with: our peace, our joy, our hope, our purpose, our blessings, and our happiness.

It was this place of emptiness that I found myself in when I gave in to the temptation of self. I tried to get back on track and fight, but I felt trapped.

I felt powerless.

I tried to do right, but then I failed.

I tried again.

Then I failed again, and again, and again.

You can handle this on your own, I thought to myself. But my sin kept taunting me, teasing me, testing me, until I finally said, "Why bother fighting it?"

Then, like a dark illusion that had made its conquest in my life, it almost immediately became a cold and aloof stranger, leaving me feeling empty, regretful, and chronically unhappy. It stole my joy, consumed my thoughts, and distracted me from the presence and promises of God, in whom true happiness resides.

We all struggle with something. And it's that area of weakness that the enemy targets every time. It doesn't matter how mature we are in Christ, how old we are, or how long we've served God; we will all be tempted. And we will all fall short at some point.

Ecclesiastes 7:20 says, "Indeed, there is no one on earth who is righteous, no one who does what is right and never sins." But that doesn't give us a free pass to do whatever we want. After all, living a life solely to fulfill *self* is like pouring water into a bucket with a hole in it. It never gets filled.

God has so many wonderful gifts and treasures for us when we obey his Word, but none of that matters unless we know *how* to obey. And let's be honest. Even when we know the *how*, we still need help understanding the *why*. As in, why do we continue to fall into the same behavior patterns that lead us away from the ways of God? The answer is found in Galatians 5:16–17:

> So I say, walk by the Spirit, and you will not gratify the desires of the flesh. For the flesh desires what is contrary to the Spirit, and the Spirit what is contrary to the flesh. They are in conflict with each other, so that you are not to do whatever you want.

We are in a war. And the battle is between our flesh (self) and the Spirit (the Spirit of God within us). The way to win the war is with our words. Why? Because our words influence what we think and, therefore, how we choose to live. The challenge is that so many of us have been sowing into the wrong team by fueling a perspective that promotes the advancement of self.

LIVING A LIFE
SOLELY TO FULFILL
SELF IS LIKE
POURING WATER
INTO A BUCKET
WITH A HOLE
IN IT. IT NEVER
GETS FILLED.

We become motivated by what we see, what we feel, and what we desire rather than what God sees, how he feels about us, and what he wants for our lives. So we open the door for the enemy to lure us with the many counterfeits that target these three self-focused motivations: the lust of the eyes, the lust of the flesh, and the pride of life. We see this played out in the biblical story of Eve encountering the serpent in the garden of Eden.

When the story opens, Eve had everything. In fact, she lacked nothing! She lived in the most beautiful garden with the most spectacular view of God's creation all around. At her fingertips were the most delightful foods created, and the coolest creatures roamed freely. And even more wonderful was the fact that the Creator himself walked alongside her and her husband, talking regularly with them. God freely gave them everything they needed and desired.

But then the enemy came in the form of a serpent. When he said that if Eve ate of the forbidden fruit she would become wise, his words implied that she *wasn't* wise, creating a fear within her that, despite all she had been given, she still lacked something. She took in the enemy's words, accepted them, and then reiterated them to Adam (Genesis 3).

She chose to trust the lies of the enemy about what she was missing and how great her life could be over the truth of God's Word. She didn't trust that God had imparted all the wisdom and knowledge necessary to live an abundant life. She was afraid of missing out.

This was the pride of life. The heart issue was *fear* rooted in a *lack of trust* in God.

When Eve saw the fruit the enemy was proffering, she told herself that it was "pleasant to the eye." She saw it, wanted it, and had to have it. The enemy lured her in by appealing to her eyes and feeding into her desires. Especially the lie that said what she had wasn't enough. She needed *more*.

The truth was that God had given her and Adam an entire garden of every kind of fruit imaginable. She already had everything, yet the enemy fed her the lie that God's everything was not enough. She felt the need for more, more, more.

This was the lust of the eyes, the heart issue at play being the desire to be *fulfilled* by things outside of God.

Then Eve told herself the forbidden fruit was "good for food." What's so bad about that, you ask? It was all about the enticement that appealed to the flesh, the feelings associated with giving in to what makes us feel good, what gives us instant gratification and even a momentary high—things such as over-indulgence of food; sexual relationships outside of marriage; outbursts of uncontrolled anger; gossip; overindulgence in alcohol, drug abuse, and more.

This was the lust of the flesh, and the heart issue here was the desire to feed into the *feel-good*, placing the flesh as a priority over the spirit.

Ever since those early days in the garden, these temptations have been a struggle for all of us. They seek to throw us off the path God has for us, which only leads to emptiness and un-happiness. But God, as we know, is a God of compassion, and he has provided a way back from this disobedience.

We find victory when we do battle against our flesh by

feeding the spirit. Just as our bodies convert food into energy, our spirits convert the Word of God into power. When we feed our bodies, we eat food, allow it to digest, then use it to take on whatever task is at hand. In the same way, when we feed our spirits, we read the Word, spend time meditating on it, then apply it to whatever situation is at hand.

As food sustains and impacts different aspects of our bodies, the Word of God sustains and transforms our spirit-man by impacting our behaviors, mind-sets, and, of course, our talk.

One of the reasons so many of us struggle and feel as if happiness has evaded us is that we've stopped leaning into the sustaining power of God's Word. Instead, we've pursued other sources and adopted certain speech, behaviors, and mind-sets that are not from God and that negatively affect how we perceive ourselves, as well as how we cope in life.

But this is not what God wants for us. Jesus Christ did not die on the cross simply so we could cope but rather so we could have an abundant life. When we readjust our hearts and begin to tell ourselves how much he loves us versus how much we think he's withholding from us, we'll begin to recognize the fulfillment of his promises rather than see only through the filter of our problems.

Jesus Christ demonstrated how to live out this readjustment of our hearts, how to use our words to fight temptation, in essence, how to talk ourselves happy. Let's take a look at Matthew 4:1–11:

> Jesus was led by the Holy Spirit to a desert. There He was
> tempted by the devil. Jesus went without food for forty

WHEN WE BEGIN
TO TELL OURSELVES
HOW MUCH GOD LOVES
US VERSUS HOW MUCH
HE'S WITHHOLDING
FROM US, WE'LL BEGIN
TO RECOGNIZE THE
FULFILLMENT OF HIS
PROMISES RATHER THAN
SEE ONLY THROUGH THE
FILTER OF OUR PROBLEMS.

days and forty nights. After that He was hungry. The devil came tempting Him and said, "If You are the Son of God, tell these stones to be made into bread."

But *Jesus said*, "It is written, 'Man is not to live on bread only. *Man is to live by every word that God speaks.*'"

Then the devil took Jesus up to Jerusalem, the holy city. He had Jesus stand on the highest part of the house of God. The devil said to Him, "If You are the Son of God, throw Yourself down. It is written, 'He has told His angels to look after You. In their hands they will hold You up. Then Your foot will not hit against a stone.'"

Jesus said to the devil, "It is written also, 'You must not tempt the Lord your God.'"

Again the devil took Jesus to a very high mountain. He had Jesus look at all the nations of the world to see how great they were. He said to Jesus, "I will give You all these nations if You will get down at my feet and worship me."

Jesus said to the devil, "Get away, Satan. It is written, 'You must worship the Lord your God. *You must obey Him only.*'" Then the devil went away from Jesus. Angels came and cared for Him. (NLV)

Notice that Jesus put himself in the same conditions that many of us find ourselves in when we fall prey to the tactics of the enemy. I don't mean being out in some wilderness; I mean being in circumstances that make us vulnerable.

Jesus was without food for forty days. His flesh was screaming to be fed. He was hungry. Many of us are hungry for certain things that gratify our flesh. We gravitate toward things that offer temporary comfort and physical relief, that give us instant gratification.

Jesus was also by himself for forty days. He was alone. Many of us feel lonely at times. We long for companionship, unity, or simply the sense of belonging. As a result, we try to fill the void of loneliness with material things, money, and even unhealthy relationships. All in an effort to feel fulfilled.

Certain conditions, such as hunger and loneliness—issues of the flesh and issues of the heart—create a perfect storm for the enemy to swoop in and take us down. But in the midst of his challenging circumstances, Jesus won and overcame. And he showed us how we can be victorious too. And it all begins with our words! Did you notice how Jesus talked himself happy when the devil sought to tempt him?

First, Jesus spoke the truth of the Word of God to combat the lies of the enemy. The only way to fight the enemy is with the power of the Word. However, we've got to *know* the Word to speak the Word! So we need to make sure we're reading it often.

Second, Jesus spoke with an assurance of knowing *who* he was, *whose* he was, and *what* he already had. Jesus knew he was the Son of God. He knew God was his Father. And he knew that all God had was his, because as the Son of God, he was heir to the things of God.

In the same way, all that God has he's also given to us, his children. We have to tell ourselves the same three things:

- *Who* we are: children of God (God's heirs).

- *Whose* we are: God is our Abba, Father.
- *What* we have: *Everything* that God has promised us. God's Word doesn't come back void, so if he said it, we have to count it done!

And finally, Jesus spoke with a certainty within his heart that whatever he was in need of, his Father would provide. God will meet every one of our needs! We just have to encourage ourselves by remembering that truth! Sometimes the best way to encourage ourselves in the Lord is by reminding ourselves of what he's done for us in the past. Since God has provided for us before, he'll provide again!

Let's focus in now on the end of the story:

Jesus said to him, "Away from me, Satan! For it is written: 'Worship the Lord your God, and serve him only.'"

Then the devil left him, and angels came and attended him.

Jesus said, *"Away from me, Satan."* What a good reminder that we have power over the enemy and our weapon is speaking the Word of God to him! The enemy is the great illusionist who tries to lure us in by telling us that the easy, sinful path will give us what it's incapable of giving, but we must remember that *he lies.* He is a defeated foe with no power over our lives. We just have to keep telling ourselves that.

"Then the devil left him . . ." Our hope is knowing that whatever we are going through, our circumstances, including our

feelings and emotions toward our circumstances, are temporary. We have to encourage ourselves by keeping the Word of God and the promises of God at the forefront of our circumstances.

The final scripture says, *"and angels came and attended him."* Other Bible versions state that the angels *ministered* to him—ministered in that they talked to him, encouraged him, and even fed him. God is so wonderful and loving that he went right to where Jesus was and attended to the main issues he was dealing with. Sure, Jesus was still in the wilderness, in that his circumstances remained the same, yet God sent help by way of his angels to attend to his issue of the flesh—hunger—and his issue of the heart—loneliness. The same love God has for his Son Jesus is the same love he has for each one of us. And it's because of that love that we can trust God is faithful and will meet all our needs.

———

Just as our heavenly Father sent angels to serve and minister to his Son following his battle with the enemy, God sent the perfect someone to minister to my heart and help me overcome my own battle with sin.

She was a warrior in every sense of the word. First of all, she was super fit and the best trainer I had ever worked with. And, second, her life was a succession of stories about fighting the good fight of faith and winning.

"The Lord put you on my heart all weekend. I'm going to train you," she said, as though I didn't have a say in the matter.

"I don't have that kind of money," I said sheepishly.

"I didn't ask you for any," she said, without blinking an eye.

A week later our training sessions began. She trained me for free. Three days a week she trained me at a country club that I couldn't afford for even one day. She sacrificed her time and money to serve me.

Our time together turned out to be a huge blessing for both of us. The outlet of exercise and the enjoyment of talking with someone about the Lord rejuvenated my body and my faith. She also loved talking about the Lord, especially since the majority of her clients either weren't Christians or simply didn't talk about their faith in God.

I'm not quite sure why I let my guard down with her, but I did. Maybe it was her kindness toward me or the fact that everything she did came out of a place of love with absolutely no expectation of payback in return. Whatever it was, it disarmed me enough to unlock the secret that had been silenced inside of me for far too long.

I didn't beat around the bush. I just told her what I had been struggling with during the past couple of months. She didn't flinch. She didn't gasp for air. And she didn't look at me as if she was appalled by my confession. She smiled gently, never looking away, and said, "I had a battle with the same thing too."

In a single moment her words released a valve within my soul and the pressure that had weighed down my heart for far too long began to subside. I felt such a tremendous relief when I opened up my mouth to tell my story. The more I shared, the more the burden lifted off my soul. The feelings of shame and guilt released out into the air with every word I spoke. From that moment on, the more I spoke of my battle, the more I felt it lose its power over me.

Funny, I thought. All this time I had been praying for God to help me and expecting him to make my sin instantaneously disappear from my life. But, clearly, God wanted me to learn something here.

James 5:16 tells us, "Therefore confess your sins to each other and pray for each other so that you may be healed. The prayer of a righteous person is powerful and effective."

We all need help. I needed help. I couldn't fight this battle alone, and God knew that. He, in his immeasurable love for me, provided the exact kind of help I needed in this season of my life. Week after week, my friend and I talked, prayed, and encouraged each other.

She never judged me.

She never used her words to condemn me.

And she never preached at me.

At times she shared her story. Other times, I shared mine. There were moments when she was brutally honest and direct with me, which I appreciated. But, most important, she loved me. And it was being on the receiving end of that kind of unconditional, nonjudgmental, steadfast love that healed me and empowered me. Her words of kindness reminded me of the power of God's love. And her words of truth set me free.

During the next couple of months I diligently got back into studying the Word, which gave me greater insight into what I was dealing with. I devoted more time to prayer, which allowed me to hear the voice of God over the voice of temptation that came out of nowhere some days. And I opened my mouth to talk more.

I definitely didn't share my struggle with everyone, but I did share it with a couple of folks I trusted who I knew would not only pray for me but would also help keep me accountable to stay away from it. Exposing it to the light, as Ephesians 5:11 says to do, took away the power of the darkness, and I found that having true friends to talk to and share my struggle with helped me know I wasn't alone, and that, with God's help, I would overcome.

While disobedience lures us away from the presence of God, obedience draws us *into* the presence of God. When we seek him, we can expect the Spirit of God to guide us in the direction we need to take in life. Just as signposts on roadways are for our safety and protection, so, too, is adhering to the Word of God within our lives.

We have to stop telling ourselves that the Bible is merely a book of "dos and don'ts." The Bible is God's love story to his children with guideposts for us to follow that were established for our benefit: to help us, protect us, guide us, and keep us within the heart of his love for us.

The more we gain an understanding of God's love for us, the more our choices will become less self-centered and more God-centered. We have to tell ourselves that our disobedience not only hurts us but, more important, hurts God. And none of

WHILE DISOBEDIENCE LURES US AWAY FROM THE PRESENCE OF GOD, OBEDIENCE DRAWS US *INTO* THE PRESENCE OF GOD.

us desire to hurt those we love. Hence, a greater understanding of the scripture, "If you love me, you will keep my commandments" (John 14:15 ESV).

When it comes to obeying the Lord, we've got to do it right away. We've got to do it God's way. And we've got to do it with a heart that reveals to him how much we love him. And when the struggle gets the best of us, we've got to shake it off and remember to tell ourselves that it's not so much about the mess-up as much as it is the get-back-up.

We all get tripped up. That's why we need Jesus and his Word to encourage ourselves and others. We must truly understand God's love for us so that when the temptation to disobey God's Word comes knocking at our door, we can talk ourselves happy by telling ourselves, "I love God more than I love Satan's counterfeit!"

> "*If you keep my commands*, you will remain in *my love*,
> just as I have kept my Father's commands and remain in
> his love. I have told you this so that *my joy may be in you*
> and that *your joy may be complete*." (John 15:10, 11)

STEPS TO TALK YOURSELF HAPPY

"I did it my way" is more than an old-time song; it's a mind-set that tends to lead us into trouble. But no matter the temptation, God has given us the tools to fight back! Take a moment to think about the following questions as you evaluate the obedience of your heart to God's Word.

- *What are those personal areas in your life that you know go against God's heart for you?* We all struggle with something and are tempted to go against the heart and Word of God every day. Rather than trying to hide your issue, go to God and ask him to help you with it.
- *What does your recurring temptation tell you about what you are afraid of?* Often, the roots of what we each struggle with personally go back to some sort of fear, whether it be fear of rejection, fear of abandonment, or fear of failure, just to name a few. Dig deep, and listen to the Holy Spirit to learn about what's underneath your struggle with certain sins. Find scriptures that address your issue, and remind yourself of what God has promised.

NOW TAKE IT, SPEAK IT, AND LIVE IT!

1. Recall how God has shown his extravagant love for you in the past. Let that encourage you to choose God over the sin.
2. Connect with a friend and ask them to be your accountability partner specifically to address the temptation you encounter over and over. Accountability is the key. We all have the tendency to hide when we know we're living outside the heart of God.
3. Don't let the enemy remind you of your failings, but instead read aloud 1 Corinthians 10:13 and remind yourself of the ways God helps you to overcome sin and temptation.

5

forgiveness

It's Time to Let It Go

"We just landed, are you here?" the text read.

They knew good and well I wasn't in Nashville for my ex-husband's funeral. I'd had no intention of going. For more than ten years I had mourned the death of our marriage. And for those same ten years I had mourned the loss of his presence in our lives. So by the time he departed this world, I felt as if I couldn't mourn any longer.

It was Friday, and the funeral was the following day. The text was the Metoyers' subtle way of broaching a very touchy subject. Their intentions were good; I knew that because they were good people. In fact, I liked them a lot. They were some of the few folks on the "other side" who had taken the time to get to know me and gain a better understanding of the truth behind my tumultuous journey with my ex-husband.

The Metoyers were one of the greatest couples I'd had the privilege to meet. They had a genuine heart for the Lord, and their kindness toward others revealed that every day. They had gone to Vanderbilt University with my ex-husband but had also been disconnected from him during the past ten or so years. That is, until his illness brought them back together. In fact, my ex's entire college clan had rallied around him during his sickness to support him. It was amazing to witness.

"If you're asking me if we're going to the funeral, we're not," I texted back, resolute in my decision.

Friends and family members were flying in from all around the country to mourn together. Funerals are a place for community grieving and unified support. But I knew that if I went, I wouldn't be privy to either. I told myself my presence would evoke nothing but anger, blame, and good ol' fashioned judgment.

For years I didn't understand why some of my random encounters with his friends and family members were so cold, and in some cases borderline hostile. It baffled me. That is, until a couple of years ago when I began to discover why.

It turned out it was *me*.

I was the reason for my ex's demise in life.

I was the reason he turned to alcohol.

I was the reason he couldn't find a job.

And I was the reason he didn't have a relationship with his son.

I was the enemy. And I destroyed his life.

It was all me.

At least that was the lie he had told everyone. To save face, he spit in mine. He used his words as a weapon to conceal the truth behind his own story by speaking lies about mine. As a result, I didn't have any relationship with his family. Neither did our son. In fact, Chase had never met them. Through the years I sent Christmas cards and pictures. I made phone calls and inquiries, but my efforts were disregarded.

I couldn't blame them. Or even be angry anymore toward them. My ex-husband's words had power. And that power had been used to destroy. It was like Solomon wrote, "Death and life are in the power of the tongue, and those who love it will eat its fruit" (Proverbs 18:21 NKJV).

The fruit of his lips was rotten because the words he spoke brought forth *death*. His lies killed relationships, stole time, and destroyed the prospect of a unified family. His words divided us. Caused dissension between us. And created hate among us.

The first time I heard that he had told everyone I wouldn't allow him to see his son, I was livid. I was so angry that it took me a long, long, *long* time to let it go.

"Are you kidding me?" I screamed. *"I'm* trying to keep him from his son? He left us! We didn't leave him! I stayed in the same house so that he could always find us. I kept the same home phone number so he could always call us. The one time he gave me the chance to talk to him during all those years, I offered to fly him from wherever he was—at least once a month—so he could see his son! I offered to pay for an apartment for him nearby so that he could be near his son! And he's telling everyone the complete opposite?"

To him, his words had been nothing more than a diversionary tactic to keep the fire off himself. He didn't realize that with every careless word, he ignited a fire that spread through the hearts of its victims, destroying all evidence of peace, harmony, and joy.

His words hurt. They hurt because they shaped the perception of the masses, creating the widespread belief that an innocent person was guilty. And that perception shaped an attitude that brought forth actions that were cruel, unkind, and uncaring.

"I really think you should come to the funeral. It will be okay," the text read.

"Okay?" I repeated sarcastically out loud.

My mind raced with thoughts: *In what world would this be okay? Why would I travel to see the people who have caused me the most grief? To honor a man who brought me the most pain? I don't want any more drama in my life! All I want is peace, the ability to take care of and protect my son, and the freedom to finally move forward so that I can close this chapter of my life.*

My emotions were on "10" and I knew I needed to pray. "Lord, I don't want to go. I don't want to face any more hurt and pain from people who don't even know me, let alone care about me and my son. I can't take it anymore, Lord. I don't want to take it anymore. Just tell me what to do. Whatever you say, I'll do."

"Please come," the text read. "Two plane tickets are at the airport for you."

———

Now if anyone has caused pain . . . *turn to forgive and comfort him,* or he may be overwhelmed by excessive sorrow. So I beg you to *reaffirm your love for him.*
(2 Corinthians 2:5–8 ESV)

Forgiveness can be a difficult pill to swallow at times. Especially when we feel that we are in the right and our offender is completely in the wrong. But carrying unforgiveness within our hearts can be lethal. There are detrimental effects unforgiveness has in a person's life spiritually, emotionally, and even physically.

Spiritually, unforgiveness separates us from God, hinders our prayers, blinds us to the things of God, and delays his promises.

Emotionally, unforgiveness breeds bitterness, sadness, anxiety, discontentment, and even depression.

Physically, unforgiveness erodes the body and, in some cases, has even proven to be a direct contributor to major illnesses, including cancers that can lead to death.

When people offend us and we choose to hold on to those offenses, it's like holding on to bricks. They're heavy and rough and create a lot of discomfort if we hold on to them long enough. And if we don't get rid of them, they pile up and create a wall that separates us from people, promises, and, most important, the presence of God. They keep us in a bottlenecked state of life.

Recently, I was in a situation where I was hurt by some friends. They wounded me to the point that I told myself they didn't deserve my forgiveness. I didn't want to let them off the hook. I wanted to keep punishing them by withholding my friendship from them.

I talked about them.

Complained about them.

And judged them.

The more negative words I spoke, the more my heart hardened toward them. By talking about it, I kept the offense alive.

And as a fire consumes, so my words consumed my peace, joy, and happiness.

During that same time, I was working on a project that should have been easy to do but was growing increasingly difficult to accomplish. I would pray and pray for God to help me, but it felt as though I was trudging through quicksand. Then one day I decided to spend the day fasting and praying about a separate matter. I needed God to move on my behalf and knew that fasting was important.

One of my closest friends and I spent the morning in prayer. As my girlfriend was praying out loud, the Lord reminded me of Mark 11:25: "And whenever you stand praying, forgive, if you have *anything against anyone*, so that your Father also who is in heaven may forgive you your trespasses" (esv).

As soon as I thought about that scripture, the Holy Spirit reminded me of my situation with the women who had hurt me. I knew I had to forgive, so I began praying for forgiveness to grow in my heart. To be candid, I did so initially just so God would give me what I was praying for.

But then, as I spoke the situation out loud, sharing my heart and my hurt with God, my words became sincere. I wanted to forgive the women, because an overwhelming love came over me for them. I knew that was the power of the Holy Spirit working to help me in my efforts to let go of the offense and forgive. He gave me the number one tool that has the power to release the stronghold of unforgiveness within our hearts: *love*.

That morning I repented and asked God to forgive me. But the process didn't stop there. Later that weekend, the Lord gave me the opportunity to meet with the main offender, the one toward whom I carried the deepest level of resentment. The Lord reminded me that the same things I had accused the women of doing, I had done to them. Gossiped, slandered, and judged.

The woman cried when I asked her to forgive me for harboring resentment toward her while behaving coldly. She hugged me and asked for forgiveness in return. It wasn't until that moment that I realized I wasn't the only one hurting. I had been so consumed with my own pain that I had neglected to acknowledge the pain of those I deemed as the offenders.

The enemy in that situation wasn't a person; the enemy came in the form of the words I spoke and believed that set the division into motion. Words of gossip, words of slander, and words of judgement.

In this situation, the Lord revealed the meaning behind James 5:16: "Therefore confess your sins to each other and pray for each other so that you may be healed. The prayer of a righteous person is powerful and effective."

We tend to go to God for his forgiveness but then neglect to go to the person we've offended or been offended by to ask for their forgiveness. Words are power, and something as simple as "Will you forgive me?" can make a world of difference in someone's life. Just as negative words can wound, hurt, and tear apart, words of kindness, encouragement, and forgiveness can heal, restore, and build up. One simple phrase like "I'm sorry" can set someone free.

My words of repentance, along with a heart of forgiveness, healed the hurt within my own heart, and that was what God wanted. He wanted to set my heart free, so that I could be free.

Forgiveness is a gift. It not only frees us from emotional bondage, it also allows the Lord to completely have free rein within our lives. On the flip side, unforgiveness is like a disease that destroys all the good that God has for us. It is like a thick smog that leaves its soot on everything.

When we explore the root of why so many people are unhappy, we can bet that somewhere down the line unforgiveness was a contributing factor. Choosing unforgiveness is not only a bottleneck that inhibits our journeys in life and the promises of God, but it also creates a bitter root that eats at our cores and breeds misery.

A woman who is one of the most miserable people I've ever met has a million reasons why her problems are everyone else's fault. She doesn't get along with her family, has a litany of broken relationships, and walks through life on the defensive. It all stems back to her childhood and the hurt she experienced at the hands of her parents.

"I'll never forgive them," she has declared.

She's always on a quest to find happiness, peace, and joy, yet they all elude her. She touts the power of crystals and follows the New Age movement. She goes to therapy and meditates daily, yet her misery never subsides.

Every chance she gets she talks about her past, which keeps her living in the past, which stirs up constant anger from the past. It's a sad cycle. She refuses to take hold of the concept that the very thing she longs for so deeply is directly linked to her unwillingness to forgive and let go.

Forgiveness is not saying that what was done was right. It doesn't justify or validate others by letting them off the hook for their words, actions, and behaviors. Forgiveness is our act of saying to God that if *he* can forgive us time and time again for all the wrong we've done against him, we can do the same for others.

Forgiveness says that we trust God and his power and we release the situation into his hands.

Forgiveness gives God the opportunity to step into the place of the offense and clean what was dirty, restore what was broken, and heal what was hurt.

Forgiveness tells the enemy that we will no longer allow our emotions and the progress of our lives to be held hostage.

———

It's easy to say that the right way to go is to forgive, but what does that look like practically? It's inevitable that we will all be offended and hurt by the actions, behaviors, and words of others at some point. When that happens, how should we handle it?

God wants us to approach offenses like a tennis match as opposed to a football game. Okay, work with me here.

In tennis, the object of the game is to hit the ball away, so our opponent can't hit it back in return. In football, the object of the game is to catch the ball, hold on tight, and try to run with it.

In football, whoever is holding on to the ball is the target. The target's opponents will do whatever they need to do to stop the target from moving forward. They will trip up, tackle, and jump on the target to try to hold that person down. That's what the enemy's goal is with us. To get us to hold on to offenses so that our lives will be hindered from all God's promises.

FORGIVENESS GIVES GOD THE OPPORTUNITY TO STEP INTO THE PLACE OF THE OFFENSE AND CLEAN WHAT WAS DIRTY, RESTORE WHAT WAS BROKEN, AND HEAL WHAT WAS HURT.

In tennis, however, when the ball comes at you, you use your racket to hit it away. The more you hit it away and prevent your opponent from responding, the more points you get until you win the match. As followers of Jesus Christ, we have to be like that! When the enemy comes at us with an offensive word or action, we've got to strike back with the Word of God. Until we win the match!

Here's the cool part about tennis. There is a unique term called "love," which refers to when a player's score is zero. What's cool is that the Lord uses the principle of love in kind of the same way.

When we ask God for forgiveness, he takes our account down to zero. He removes all evidence of our misdeeds, offenses, and sins by calling them nil, nothing, and nonexistent. Love not only covers a multitude of sin, love washes all evidence of our sins away. God says, "I am he who blots out your transgressions for my own sake, and I will not remember your sins" (Isaiah 43:25 ESV).

In the same way the love of Jesus Christ does that for us, time and time again, we must do that for one another. By forgiving one another—removing all accounts from one another. And the key is to stop using our words to keep the offenses alive. We've got to stop talking about them.

Happiness is the ability to forgive and be forgiven while choosing to allow love to cover the offense, so we can let it go for good.

"Lord, how often will my brother sin against me, and
I forgive him? As many as seven times?" Jesus said to
him, "I do not say to you seven times, but seventy-seven
times." (Matthew 18:21–22 ESV)

When it came to forgiving my ex-husband I found I just
couldn't do it. Every time God helped me take that wall of unforgiveness down, my ex-husband would do something that
made it go back up. I tried for years to forgive him, but my
words were empty.

"Sure, I've forgiven him," I would often tell people, but the
truth within my heart told a different story.

I tried.

I wanted to.

But I couldn't.

I couldn't, because every time I thought about him or talked
about him I would get infuriated all over again. I wanted justice,
and for the first couple of years after he left us I wanted him to
pay for all the hurt he had caused me.

The thorn in my flesh had very little to do with all the issues
within our marriage; the big offense was how—in my eyes—his
actions, choices, and especially his lies had changed the course
of my life and my son's life forever.

I hated that I had been stripped of the opportunity to have a
successful marriage with a loving husband and several children.

I hated that I had to face every problem on my own without
the support of a helpmate.

And I hated that I was thrown back into the wolves'

den known as the dating game, a situation that made me feel vulnerable, unprotected, and unsafe.

I told myself that my ex-husband had left us weak, positioned us as targets, and made us people to be pitied. Every time I made any progress toward letting it go, something or someone would spark a memory that would bring to life the whole set of offenses all over again. I remember sitting at home or in my office replaying hurtful conversations and painful moments over and over in my mind. The words we spoke to each other were revived as I repeated them to whoever was willing to listen.

The anger would rise up in me like a sleeping monster, and it would take me quite a while to settle down again. I talked about the offenses. I thought about the offenses. I believed wholeheartedly I was the victim in every offense, and for that I was more than angry. I had grown bitter.

I told myself that everyone else was married, but because of him I wasn't.

I told myself that everyone else had a family, but because of him my options were now limited.

And I told myself that true happiness eluded me, because he had taught me I could never trust anyone ever again.

Day after day, seeds of hatred toward my ex-husband grew in my heart. The more I spoke of the hate, the more my heart carried the burden of the hate. I knew I should forgive. I understood it was a requirement of God to forgive. But for a long time, I didn't feel that my ex-husband deserved my forgiveness.

"Forgiveness is for you, not so much for the other person,"

my friends would say. "It will set you free from all the hurt and pain that you're choosing to carry, Kristi."

I knew they were right. And on most days I tried. That is, until he did something that made me angry all over again. There was always this pressure, especially as a Christian in the public eye, to be a saint. Forgive everything, love everybody, and never get angry about anything. I tried. I mean, I really tried. But I just couldn't do it.

At one point I remember wanting to hold on to the anger a little longer, because, in a strange way, I enjoyed it. I found a strange sense of comfort in relishing my anger toward him. But then something happened. Two years had gone by, and my ex-husband was long gone, living his own life somewhere. No contact, no child support, and no acknowledgement of what he had left behind.

I don't know what triggered it, but one day I discovered I suddenly didn't want to hold on to my anger anymore. I no longer cared about who was right or who was wrong. I just wanted to be free from the weight of it all.

But the weight had grown too heavy, and I couldn't lift it off on my own. I needed the Lord to get down into the depths of my heart so that he could pull out the deep root of bitterness that had grown and established itself by the watering of my own words. So, this time, rather than using my words to complain about my husband, I used my words to pray for him.

Then I asked the Lord to do what I was incapable of doing.

"I need you to help me, Lord. I need you to do it for me,

Jesus. You have the power to do anything, and there is nothing impossible for you. *So, will you forgive him through me?"*

"Will you forgive him through me?"

Those were the words I had never spoken before, yet those were the words that set me free. That afternoon when I prayed, no lightning bolts came through the ceiling. And no choir of angels started to sing. In fact, nothing happened. But that was the coolest part of all. It was in the *nothing* where I saw that God did everything!

Nothing hurt anymore.

Nothing made me sad anymore.

And *nothing* sparked that anger, because the Holy Spirit took it all away. When we step aside and allow the Holy Spirit to step in, we will see the impossible become possible.

"If the Son sets you free, you will be free indeed" (John 8:36).

I knew for certain God had set me free from unforgiveness when someone told me something about my ex-husband and I wasn't bothered. The tightness in my chest and the fire in my belly that usually came when his name was mentioned was completely gone. The love that I once felt for him had also changed.

As I committed to pray for him, stopped talking negatively about him, and chose to leave the old offenses behind by refusing to dwell on them, a new love rekindled for him. Not a romantic kind of love, but more like brotherly love. When it came to praying for him, some days were easier than others, but the Holy Spirit definitely guided me along the way.

The greatest part about forgiving the seemingly unforgivable

WHEN WE STEP
ASIDE AND ALLOW
THE HOLY SPIRIT
TO STEP IN, WE
WILL SEE THE
IMPOSSIBLE
BECOME POSSIBLE.

is the testimony you can share when someone denies the feasibility to forgive by saying, "It's easier said than done." Now, because of my own experience, I can say with conviction, there is hope. There is hope in knowing that with God all things are possible. And not just possible, workable.

The key is in the how: praying for the guidance of the Holy Spirit, letting go, and making sure your prayers reflect the forgiveness that can only come through God. In this way, we will never again allow another person to steal our *joy*!

———

The funeral was in less than twenty-four hours, and I was running around frantically to get Chase and me ready for the flight that took off in five hours.

By the time we got to our hotel it was almost midnight, and I was already emotionally drained.

"What in the world are you doing?" I reprimanded myself as I lay in the hotel bed next to my sleeping son. Inside I was an emotional wreck, but I was doing everything in my power to seem calm for my son.

I hadn't known how he was going to respond when I picked him up from school earlier that day to tell him that we were on our way to the airport to go to his father's funeral. While the situation was a challenge for me, it proved to be much more difficult for my son.

When he had first met his father several months before, he had been excited and understandably nervous. And while the initial meeting went great, the following days proved difficult. Chase's image of what his dad would be like was shattered. He wasn't impressed.

My ex-husband's illness had not only affected his physical appearance but also his state of mind. He was sometimes snappy and agitated. His words were often critical, and his conversations made very little sense. What I hated the most was that he still lied.

"Lie to me. Lie to everyone else. But don't lie to our son," I said one day over the phone before he blocked me. When we had been married, he had lied so much that when I had my son I named him Chase, which means "pursuer of the truth." Ever since Chase was a baby, I've instilled in him the importance of speaking the truth no matter what.

My son wasn't accustomed to someone lying to him. So, when his father said, "I'll give you . . ." or "I'll call you" or "I'll do this for you . . ." and his words were not fulfilled, let's just say it wasn't a good thing. I didn't realize the magnitude of the effect his father's lies had on him until a couple of months after the visit.

I asked Chase to send a friendly text to tell his dad we were thinking about him, and Chase's response surprised me.

"Do I have to?" he asked.

"Sure. Why not?"

"I don't want to."

"Why?" I was confused. Then the very thing I feared the most came pouring out of my son. An anger I hadn't seen in him since he was six years old and came home from school mad that all the other children had fathers and he didn't.

"He's a liar, Mom. Everything he says is a lie. He promises stuff but never does it. And I hate what he does to you. Since he came back into our lives, you've been all stressed out and not really that happy anymore."

Then he added the kicker.

"I wish I had never met him. I wish he had never come back into our lives."

My heart bled for Chase. At one point I had wrestled with those same feelings, so I wasn't certain how to address these issues with my son.

I sat next to him on his bedroom floor looking into his face as angry tears streamed down his cheeks. He was no longer a little boy but a young man growing into manhood. He watched and listened to every word spoken around him, and with time he had gathered the truth about his father's life and choices. His reaction provided clues as to how it was impacting his heart.

I reached out to hug him while begging God to give me his wisdom about what I should do.

For months after that day, I noticed a change in my son. His heart was hardening, and a root of bitterness was starting to develop toward his father. Every night I prayed for God to help him, yet every day I saw my son morph into a child I no longer recognized. He was angry, bitter, and hardened.

"Help him, Jesus. Heal him, Lord. Remove every negative word spoken by his father, or about his father, from Chase's heart. Heal him, Lord, and help him forgive his father. Lord, will you do it now so that this doesn't stay with him as he grows into an adult?"

God is faithful, and he answered my prayer on May 24, 2015, Pentecost Sunday. During the church service while the worship team was leading, the presence of the Holy Spirit fell on the congregation as never before. I heard the Lord speak to my heart.

He said, "Put your hand on Chase."

I placed my hand on my son's back while continuing to worship God. I don't know what he did or how he did it; all I know is that the Lord delivered my son. By his power and might, his love went into the depth of Chase's heart and removed every trace of bitterness, anger, and unforgiveness toward his father. By the end of that church service, the tenderness and softness had returned. Praise the Lord!

But now, here we were in Nashville. The funeral was in a couple of hours, and I was chickening out. I got on the phone with my sister.

"Mindi. I made a huge mistake. I've got to get out of here. Will you call the airline and see if you can get us on a flight back home? I can't go to the funeral. I can't face the people my ex-husband lied to for years about me. I just can't take anymore beat-downs in life. Especially not in this season with everything that's happened."

"Okay, I'll call you right back."

By now I was pacing in the hotel room, feeling trapped. I wanted out so badly that I was thinking about renting a car to drive us home.

I lunged at the phone when I heard it ring.

"Sorry. There are no flights until Sunday morning. You might as well bite the bullet and go to the funeral, Kristi. You'll be okay."

I sat on the side of the bed, devastated but resolving myself to do what I needed to do.

"Kristi, do it for Chase. He's never met his other grand-mother or his aunts and uncles. Do it for him. Take the bullet for him," I said to myself.

The wonderful couple who had finagled me into making the trip to Nashville were standing outside of the church waiting for us when we arrived. Chase was calm, and I was a nervous wreck. My strategy was to go in late, sit in the back, then leave early before anyone noticed.

"You ready?" the Metoyers asked.

"We've got you. You're going to be okay," they assured me as they walked in front of us into the church, acting as a blockade between me and the incoming grenades I was anticipating.

The church was a typical old black Baptist church with wooden pews and a tall white steeple. As we walked in, my eyes went to the first row where my ex-husband's entire family sat. I hadn't seen most of them for more than seventeen years, since our wedding day. I was aiming for the back row when our party continued to walk down the narrow church aisle.

My heart was racing and my temperature rising; I could feel the stares drilling holes in my back. Even if people didn't know me personally, most knew of me since my ex-husband was mar-ried to "the girl on *The 700 Club*." I squeezed Chase's hand as if to gain support from him rather than the other way around.

Then it happened.

My ex-mother-in-law turned her head and saw me. With a loud gasp she cupped her hand over her mouth and said, "Oh, my God!"

One by one, everyone in the family turned to look at me and my son standing frozen in the middle of the aisle.

Do I run? Do I stay and fight? What do I do? I thought frantically to myself. Then, as if we were in a Tyler Perry movie, the entire front row stood up. Everything went into slow motion as I heard screams and gasps and they came lunging toward us.

My ex-husband's mother was the first to get in my face and say, "*I beg you to forgive me.* I'm *so* sorry for everything that I've done to you, said about you, thought about you. Will you forgive me?"

Before I could respond, one of my ex-husband's sisters moved in and took hold of both of my arms. She was crying and visibly shaking. "Kristi, I am so sorry. I was wrong for everything that I said about you. I was wrong. *Please forgive me.*"

I was in shock. Everybody was hugging me. Kissing on my son and crying and laughing all at the same time. It was all so surreal. Especially for them, since before them stood the spitting image of their son and their brother in the form of Chase. He looked just like his father.

In one single moment, God mended everything with the simple words, "Will you forgive me?"

Time that was lost was found.

Relationships that were broken were mended.

And hearts that were wounded were healed.

Their words acted as a healing salve to my soul. And their words gave us something that we all longed for: true happiness!

> How happy he is whose wrong-doing is forgiven,
> and whose sin is covered! How happy is the man whose

sin the Lord does not hold against him, and in whose spirit there is nothing false. (Psalm 32:1–2 NLV)

STEPS TO TALK YOURSELF HAPPY

One of the greatest obstacles we all will have to face and overcome is the act of forgiveness. The hope is knowing that God has given us the power to forgive anything through the Holy Spirit. As we walk this journey of forgiveness, let's take inventory of our hearts with the questions below.

- *Who do you need to forgive?* As God brings someone to mind, ask him to help you forgive that person. You can say out loud, "Lord, will you forgive _____ through me?" And you can know that God will do it for you.
- *Are you a tennis player or football player?* If you answered football player, then ask the Lord to teach you how to stop holding on to and instead release offenses so that you can be set free.

NOW TAKE IT, SPEAK IT, AND LIVE IT!

1. Make the decision to stop talking about past offenses so that you can allow the Lord to heal your heart and relieve the pain from hurtful memories.

2. If you are the offender in someone's life, take the bold step of meeting with them and saying, "Will you forgive me?"

3. Read Ephesians 1:7 out loud and remember the price Jesus paid to offer all of us forgiveness. In light of this gift, choose to let your offenses go and walk in the freedom God desires for you.

6

praise

Find Joy in the Presence of God

It was January 2004, and my ex-husband had recently walked out for good. I sat in my driveway completely numb, trying to muster enough strength to get out of the car. It was pitch black outside.

My mother greeted me at the door with my chubby little three-month-old baby in her arms. I reached out to take him and held him tightly, as if I was holding on to a life jacket. Neither my mother nor I said a word, but the expressions on our faces spoke volumes. I walked into the family room and sat on the couch where my dad was watching an old black-and-white cowboy movie on the television.

"Well?" my mother said softly, as if trying not to disrupt the sorrow gradually filling the room. "How did the meeting go?"

"Okay, I guess. They were sympathetic and understanding," I mumbled. "They suggested that it may be best for me to step down as a cohost of *The 700 Club*." Tears were stinging my eyes as I heard the words fall like bricks out of my mouth.

"With the new baby and the situation with my husband leaving . . . It's a lot, and they just want to make sure I'm okay."

My words trailed off as I looked down at my little baby. I wasn't clear whether this situation with my job was temporary or permanent, but regardless, it was the final punch that took me down.

I was done.

I was past discouraged.

I was defeated.

I handed the baby over to my dad while I went into my bathroom. I just wanted to be alone. All lights were off except for a dim light peering through the crack from the adjoining room. Although my bathtub was large I sat on one side, knees pressed in to my chest, my body curled up into a ball. I was trying to prevent any more blows from attacking my heart.

My life was in the middle of a storm, and it felt as if everything was hitting all at once.

My husband leaving.

Raising a newborn on my own.

The discovery of empty bank accounts.

And now, the uncertainty of a career I had invested in for years.

One word kept running over and over in my mind. *Failure.* I told myself that I had failed in my marriage.

Failed in my faith.

Failed in my ministry.

And even failed my son.

"I am a failure," I said, only loud enough for my ears to hear.

The dialogue within my mind made the room grow darker

as the words I held on to gradually sucked away the remaining hope that lingered within my heart.

"I should have prayed more and believed more. My faith should have been stronger. Then maybe my marriage wouldn't have failed. I get why they removed me from my position in ministry. Who am I to minister to anyone? And my son. I've failed him too. I failed to give him the same kind of two-parent, strong Christian home I grew up in. Now, I'm nothing more than a statistic. Another black woman raising her black child on her own."

Just then, I glanced down at my belly that was still misshapen from having given birth. My body looked foreign. Stretch marks and saggy skin now covered my usually tight abs and hips. It was all so symbolic. I couldn't see the beauty in the story that my body displayed. All I saw was the disfigurement and permanent scars. As I inspected every flaw, all I could say to myself was, "I'm broken. I'm damaged. I'm used goods. Who is ever going to want me now?"

The knock on the bathroom door momentarily jolted me out of my pity party. It was my mother carrying a warm cup of milk and a small plate of toast. I could see by the glint of her eyes that she had been crying. They had that glassy look from the tears that pooled around them. Sensing that I needed to be alone, she placed the cup and platter at the edge of the tub, kissed me on my cheek, and walked out.

"I love you," she said as she paused to look at me before closing the door.

"I love you, too, Mom."

When I crawled into bed that night, I curled up into a fetal position. I felt so miniscule compared to the magnitude of my issues. I was scared they would break me. My heart was so heavy, I couldn't pray. I wanted to pray, but I was too distraught to form the words. Besides, I had convinced myself the circumstances within my life had deemed me a failure in the eyes of God as well. And if that was the case, I doubted God would listen to the prayers of someone like me anyway.

So, I decided to cage my words. I was tired of talking. After all, for months every conversation had begun and ended with the bad going on in my life. Talking only about the bad forced me to see only the bad. And constantly seeing the bad made me feel, well, bad.

Sometimes it seems as if those times in our lives that are filled with one difficult thing after another are just what they look like on the surface: bad. No redeeming qualities. Simply bad. But the truth is, it's through our challenges that we gain a deeper insight into the heart, the ways, and the Word of God.

It's in the *secret place*—that quiet, gut-honest, one-on-one place where we look God in the eye, pour out our hearts, listen for his whisper, and begin to praise him again—that we learn dependency on God and gain a greater understanding of how God is trustworthy in every aspect of our lives.

The psalmist put it this way:

> He who dwells in the secret place of the Most High
> Shall abide under the shadow of the Almighty.

I will say of the LORD, "He is my refuge and my fortress;
My God, in Him I will trust." (Psalm 91:1–2 NKJV)

So many things come out of our trials and tribulations. In fact, it's often in the difficult times that we realize we have nothing without the presence and power of God. We learn things about ourselves that we were most likely unaware of, including things we are capable of, driven by, and get tripped up on. All things that God reveals to us so we can go to him for help.

More often than not, what we discover are mind-sets, perspectives, and behavior patterns that have been stumbling blocks, preventing us from obtaining all God's promises for our lives. God's heart is for us to see them and repent of them, so we can become free of them.

When we feel as if life is falling apart and our issues begin to bubble to the surface, God wants to draw our attention back to him. Regardless of what sends us into the presence of God, though, it's important to get into his presence and learn what it is to praise him in the midst of our pain. Because in his presence is hope, restoration, and redemption.

At this, Job got up and tore his robe and shaved his head. Then he fell to the ground in *worship* and said: "Naked I came from my mother's womb, and naked I will depart. The LORD gave and the LORD has taken away; *may the name of the LORD be praised.*" (Job 1:20–21)

IT'S OFTEN IN THE
DIFFICULT TIMES
THAT WE REALIZE
WE HAVE NOTHING
WITHOUT THE
PRESENCE AND
POWER OF GOD.

Job. It's the one book in the Bible many of us are reluctant to read. After all, it's kind of a killjoy. In fact, Job's story is downright tragic. In one fell swoop he lost almost everything valuable to him.

He lost all ten of his children by a freak act of nature.

He lost his property by an act of violence.

And he lost his health by the direct hand of the enemy.

Job's story makes no sense! By God's own account, Job was "a blameless and upright man, one who fears God and shuns evil" (Job 1:8 NKJV). With a glowing description like that, Job should have been untouchable. Yet, God allowed him to face immeasurable suffering, unimaginable heartbreak, and incapacitating loss. Why?

When bad things happen it's easy to ask God *why*? But the greater question might be, *how*?

How does God want us to respond?

How can we find our way through the rough patches?

And *how* can we experience joy in the midst of our sorrow?

When we read Job's story, at first the answer isn't very clear. But then, through Job's *talk*, we learn the heart of the story and the lessons God wants us to learn when we, too, are facing life's most challenging moments.

Immediately, Job gives us the answer: "The LORD gave and the LORD has taken away; *may the name of the LORD be praised*" (Job 1:21).

Job didn't use his words to complain to God or blame God, but instead his immediate response was to praise and worship God. How insanely uncommon is that? He worshipped, laid prostrate before God, and reverenced him. Job praised and blessed God by using his words to show his adoration and trust in God.

Praising God is the last thing most of us want to do when we feel that life is beating us down. It makes no logical sense to rejoice in the Lord when we're in the fire. And if some of us are *really* honest with ourselves, we'll admit that it's easier to use our words to question God—or, dare I say, even blame God—than it is to thank him! Especially when we feel that God could have or should have protected us from something.

But that's just it. Praise allows us to see beyond our own limited view and forces us to speak to and to speak about the only One who has the full view of our situation and has the power to do something about it. Praise, or the act of rejoicing in the Lord, opens the door and ushers us into the presence of God. Why? Because God inhabits our praises (Psalm 22:3).

Praise, with a heart of thanksgiving, walks us right into the throne room of the King of kings and the Lord of lords.

Praise acknowledges the immeasurable gifts found in the promises of his Word.

Praise allows us to shift our perspective from our problems onto the problem solver.

Praise gives us hope.

Praise ushers us into the freedom found only in Christ.

And, finally, true praise is when we align our hearts, minds, and mouths to express the outpouring of our love toward our God, because praise brings God joy. And not just joy—praise makes God happy. And that, in turn, makes us happy, no matter our circumstance.

Praise is the key. But let's be honest, how many of us respond to challenges that way? I have missed the mark on this principle many times. In fact, I completely failed that test when my husband left us so alone. The only words that came out of my mouth were choice words that I later had to repent for. And, worse yet, not only did I not praise God in my situation, I used my words to question God by asking him why he would allow me to marry a man who would hurt me so deeply.

But this wasn't Job's reaction. The Bible says, "In all this Job did not sin with his lips . . . nor charge God with wrong" (Job 2:10; 1:22 NKJV). In other words, he didn't blame God or even question God. Job made a conscious decision to guard his words; he made a concerted effort to refrain from speaking words that went against the truth of God's Word.

Why was it so important that Job did not sin with his lips? Because Job understood the power and impact his words had on directing his outlook and the course of his life. Job needed to talk himself happy just to survive. Well, maybe not quite *happy* initially, but without a doubt, he needed to talk himself hopeful. After all, the folks around him, who were supposed to support him, ended up blaming him, accusing him, and even chastising him for being in the situation he was in.

"My relatives have failed, and my close friends have forgotten me" (Job 19:14 NKJV).

"Those whom I love have turned against me" (Job 19:19 NKJV).

PRAISE ALLOWS
US TO SHIFT OUR
PERSPECTIVE
FROM OUR
PROBLEMS
ONTO THE
PROBLEM SOLVER.

Isn't that just like some people? Rather than offering mercy or compassion, they throw judgment, legalism, and blame in your face by saying things like, "You must have done something wrong for all this to be happening to you."

Shortly after my husband left me, the wife of a man I worked with came to me and said, "Why would you have a baby if your marriage was so bad that your husband left you?"

I wanted to throw her down on the floor and shove my foot in her mouth to shut her up. I was so upset by her cruel and insensitive comment that I later went home and cried. Not because I was hurt, but because I was angry. During the time when I needed words of encouragement the most, I had to bear the additional weight of her malicious words of judgment.

As Job's story unfolded, Job's friends pretty much did the same thing. They stomped all over him with their words of accusation. But it is the words that came out of his wife's mouth that strike me the most.

"Do you still hold fast to your integrity? Curse God and die!" Job's wife said to him (Job 2:9 NKJV). That's crazy! But this is a perfect example of how sometimes the ones we love the most speak words that hurt us the deepest. It may not be as heart-wrenching as "Curse God and die!" but the impact of their words damage our hearts all the same. They influence how we see ourselves and the condition of our lives. Words such as: "You'll never be . . . You can't do . . . You won't ever. . . . You're nothing. You're stupid. You're a mistake."

Job's closest friends and his own wife used their words to harm rather than to heal, because all they perceived was what they could physically see. We will all experience the same hurt at one point or another. Many of us may have to deal with added pressure and increased disappointment when we expect our loved ones to respond in one way, but they respond in the opposite.

What should we do when that happens? We should do what Job did:

> But he said to her, "You speak as one of the foolish women would speak. *Shall we receive good from God, and shall we not receive evil?" In all this Job did not sin with his lips.* (Job 2:10 ESV)

Job chose to reject the negative words spoken by his wife and his friends by embracing the truth of what he knew about God. He told himself who God was, along with what God would do for him. In other words, he encouraged himself in the Lord! And, as a result, he built his faith on knowing that God was going to save him (Job 13:16) and vindicate him (Job 13:18).

Throughout Job's story, Job's friends talked.

Job's wife talked.

Job even talked.

But it wasn't until God spoke that Job's life turned around. Since Job had chosen to praise and worship God in the midst of his challenge, he was positioned before the Lord to hear directly from him when he spoke.

In chapter 38 God begins to reveal his omnipotence, his unlimited power, to Job. Job was like many of us. His understanding of God was primarily based on what he had *heard* of God. But it wasn't until God spoke, reiterating all that he is, can do, and will do by his unlimited power, that Job's heart was transformed. This had to happen before any of Job's circumstances changed.

Through the spoken Word of God, Job went from understanding the things of God to knowing firsthand the things of God. And from that place of knowing, Job was able to find his happy in the midst of his heartbreak.

Job's revelation was expressed best in chapter 42, verses 1 through 5:

Then Job replied to the LORD:

> "*I know that you can do all things;*
>   no purpose of yours can be thwarted.
> You asked, 'Who is this that obscures my plans
>   without knowledge?'
>   Surely I spoke of things I did not understand,
>   things too wonderful for me to know.
>
> "You said, 'Listen now, and I will speak;
>   I will question you,
>   and you shall answer me.'
> *My ears had heard of you*
>   *but now my eyes have seen you.*"

Job saw God! He saw God because he was in the presence of God. He positioned himself there when he praised him. The advantage of being in such close proximity to God is that as Job spoke, God heard him—and not only heard him but responded to him. That interaction with God allowed Job to witness God's power in the midst of his struggle and God's greatness in the midst of his grief.

Our words have to be about more than giving ourselves pep talks or reciting what we've heard from others. Our words must serve a purpose.

A purpose to rekindle the faith within our hearts.

A purpose to remind ourselves of the things of God.

And a purpose to position ourselves in the throne room of our heavenly Father.

Our words must reflect our praise and worship of God and place him before ourselves, recognizing his sovereignty above our circumstances. This is the lesson God wants us to learn about the power of our words. By keeping his Word at the forefront of our minds, thoughts, and hearts, we encourage ourselves and others, creating life and infusing hope into our situations!

By the end of the book, Job's tone changed from that of a man who thought he had all the answers to the tone of a man who recognized that he was nothing and had control of nothing outside of the presence of God.

After asking God to forgive him, he then did what God would have us to do. He forgave and prayed for the people who had used their words against him. Words that were aimed to take him further down rather than to lift him up. The heart transformation he'd experienced in the presence of the Lord propelled him to this unselfish act of love. And then the Lord moved on his behalf.

OUR WORDS
HAVE TO BE ABOUT
MORE THAN GIVING
OURSELVES PEP
TALKS OR RECITING
WHAT WE'VE
HEARD FROM
OTHERS.

After Job had prayed for his friends, the LORD restored his fortunes and gave him twice as much as he had before. (Job 42:10)

———

> May my lips overflow with praise,
>   for you teach me your decrees.
> May my tongue sing of your word,
>   for all your commands are righteous.
> May your hand be ready to help me,
>   for I have chosen your precepts.
>   (PSALM 119:171–173)

It was a little more than a year before I could get to the place in my heart where I could speak the words of Job: "Though He slay me, yet will I trust Him" (Job 13:15 NKJV) and "The LORD gave, and the LORD has taken away; Blessed be the name of the LORD" (Job 1:20–21 NKJV). I didn't know what to expect day after day, but I told myself that I would trust God no matter what and praise him in the process.

While my life was not unfolding as I would have liked it to, God was walking me through the rough patches every single day. My marriage was still over and my bank accounts still empty, but I was praising God I at least *had* a paycheck.

I did step down from cohosting but continued working behind the scenes as a television producer. After six months I was even asked to resume my on-air role by taking a seat back in the hosting chair on Mother's Day. Another example of God's plan of redemption in my life.

I was living in this place of dependence on God and praise when the court papers showed up at the front door. I had to catch my breath for a moment when I first saw them. This was it. Our final court date for the divorce. Virginia law splits everything in half.

I knew I was going to lose the house. My ex had already taken all our money, so there was nothing to split there. I didn't care about anything inside the house except my clothes and photo albums. He had already hijacked our computer and other random things, but I didn't care anymore. He could take it all. I just wanted one thing: the assurance that my son would be safe and okay.

For most of the year I hadn't seen my ex-husband. He was like a phantom in the night who left no trace at all. The first couple of months he'd stopped by the house once or twice just to pick up his mail, but for the most part, he'd had little to no dealing with us.

No child support.

No visits.

No phone calls.

No acknowledgment.

At first, I was ticked off and prayed relentlessly that God would change his heart and bring him back to us. Those few times I saw him I vied for his attention or forced baby Chase on him. He played the game just long enough to have me take pictures of him and the baby as proof to his friends of his fabricated life with us. But it was all a lie. A game to pacify the onlookers for as long as he could keep up the ruse.

As I took a mental note of the court date, which was a couple of weeks away, I could feel my heart pounding.

"Lord," I prayed, "I thank you for taking care of this situation as you've always taken care of me and my son. Lord, I praise you and thank you that I can trust in you. Lord, I praise you for your goodness and your grace and thank you for your favor in this situation."

In that moment, a calm came over me as I continued to think about the goodness of God and how I was going to trust him no matter the outcome.

Weeks later, I sat with my dad and my lawyer at the magistrate's office. My ex-husband had skipped out on the previous three court dates we had set, and now we were here again. My parents had dropped everything and driven more than seven hours each way to support me. We waited for twenty minutes.

I had not fully understood the effect the situation had on my parents until I was sitting in the magistrate's office that day. As we waited for my soon-to-be ex-husband to arrive, the counsel asked me to identify all parties present. When I said my father's full name, my dad spoke up for the first time. With fire in his eyes, he looked at the counsel and said, "I gave my daughter to this man who vowed to take care of her. He didn't, so I'm here to do the job."

Everyone in the room paused, taking in the authority behind my father's words.

I could hear the ticking from the clock on the wall and the jostling of the papers from my file. I looked at my dad for comfort and some kind of reassurance. He looked right back at me with an undeniable love yet with a face void of a smile. He had this look like he meant business and no one was ever going to mess with his daughter again.

I thought about how my father's presence in this situation was symbolic of God's presence in my life. My dad had positioned himself right by my side as if to take all the bullets for me. No matter what, he was going to protect me, fight for me, and restore me. My father's love was steadying and reminded me of God's goodness and steadfast love for me, even in the worst of situations. It was in that moment I determined that regardless of the verdict, I was going to praise God for his faithfulness.

My ex-husband never showed up. For the fourth time in a row. Eventually the counselor ruled the verdict.

Minutes. That's all it took. Just a few minutes and a couple of signatures, and everything changed.

The car.

The deed to the house.

Everything in the house.

The baby.

God took care of everything in my favor.

I thought of Job's proclamation of faith: "I know that my redeemer lives" (Job 19:25). Redeemer, as in Jesus Christ. The one who saves, sets free, and restores what was lost. This was a truth I had personally come to know all the way down to my bones, and though it was a bittersweet moment, I found happiness in the midst of it.

But here's the deal: happiness isn't found in one's triumph over another's tragedy. Or one's win or over another's loss. Happiness is simply trusting God with every aspect of our lives by acknowledging his hand at work.

We have to praise God no matter what we're going through, because praise ushers us into the presence of God. In Philippians 4, the apostle Paul talks about being content in all things. When life is good, bad, ugly, or indifferent, we must praise God. Not merely for the good of what we see or even the good of what we hope for, but because we know we have a redeemer who loves us, brings life out of death, and is good, *always!*

> The Lord gives me a reason to be full of joy. . . . I have learned to be *happy* with whatever I have. I know how to get along with little and how to live when I have much. I have learned the secret of being happy at all times. If I am full of food and have all I need, I am happy. If I am hungry and need more, I am happy. I can do all things because Christ gives me the strength. (Philippians 4:10–13 NLV)

STEPS TO TALK YOURSELF HAPPY

Praise ushers us into the presence of God, so we must use our voices to praise him often. Praise is not always an easy path to walk, especially when life seems full of heavy burdens. But we must remember that in his presence is where we find true joy! So let's take inventory of our hearts as we think about worshipping God in the midst of pain.

- *What are some of the different characteristics of God?* Think on those characteristics, and use your words to

HAPPINESS IS
SIMPLY TRUSTING
GOD WITH
EVERY ASPECT
OF OUR LIVES BY
ACKNOWLEDGING
HIS HAND AT WORK.

praise him for them. Research the different names of God and see how much you learn about who God is based upon what name he has!

- *What are some of your favorite ways that you have seen God move in your life?* When we find ourselves too burdened to praise and worship, it's sometimes because our thoughts are too closely focused on our circumstances, making it difficult for us to see the big picture of our lives. It's helpful to pull back, remember how God has come through, see what he is already doing, and praise him for what he will do in the future.

NOW TAKE IT, SPEAK IT, AND LIVE IT!

1. Go into the secret place, and pour your heart out to God. Give him everything: your fears, concerns, anxieties, everything—because when you give all of yourself, he will give all of himself to you.
2. Think about the omnipotence—the unlimited power—of God. Take a moment to reflect on the magnitude of who God is and the amazing fact that this all-powerful God loves and cares for you in every situation in your life, no matter how small. Remind yourself that he can do anything and you can trust him to come through for you.
3. Put on some worship music and just begin to sing. Sing until your heart begins to lift. Sing praise and worship songs to God until those words of truth get down into your heart and lift your spirit. Just sing!

7

help

Discover the Power of Community

"I have *no* clue what I'm doing," I said to God, just in case he didn't know.

I've always been more of the creative type. I'm not a business kind of person. Dealing with numbers gives me hives, and the thought of putting together a business plan is like saying, "Go learn Japanese by tomorrow." It's not very plausible.

Yet here I was, every sign pointing in the direction of me starting my own company. The mere thought of having to do everything on my own gave me heart palpitations.

"I *can't* do this, Lord. I don't know *how* to do this, Lord. I don't even think I'm *capable* of doing this, Lord."

I'd had a plan for my life, and my plan had involved working for someone else. All I wanted to do was show up, do my job, and let the burden of running a company fall on someone else's shoulders. After all, that was safe, comfortable, and familiar. Sure, it would be cool to have my own gig where I could call the shots and walk out my own vision, but that wasn't me.

"Let me just stay in my lane and let someone else take the lead. I'm comfortable staying where I am and doing what I know to do," I said to God. But I didn't realize that my reluctance to go where God was leading me was preventing me from experiencing some incredible blessings he had in store!

The truth was that I needed help. I needed someone to show me the way. I needed someone to help me get past, well, me. I was dealing with so many personal hang-ups and insecurities that I had become paralyzed in my disbelief that God could use me in this new arena. I believed God could do amazing things through others, but me? Not so much.

It's such a miserable and helpless feeling when we find ourselves in situations where we are simply unable to handle them on our own. It's that place of vulnerability where, although we do everything we know to do, we still feel as though we can't keep afloat. We sink deeper and deeper, pulled down by the weight of what we're facing until everything just goes black. That's a lot like how it feels to drown. I should know, because I've almost drowned on three separate occasions.

The first time, I was about three or four years old, and we were at a family friend's home playing in their pool. Someone put me into one of those round inflatable inner tubes with a seat attached in it. Everything was fine until one of the kids jumped in, doing a cannonball and creating a huge wave that knocked my little inner tube over. With my legs still confined in the plastic seat, I thrashed and wiggled my body to free myself but couldn't. Although there were many people close by, no one seemed to notice. Help was less than an arm's length away but everyone was too involved in their lives to notice what was happening in mine. I was in the midst of a crowd and yet I was drowning.

The second time I almost drowned I was around six years old. My family was on vacation, and I begged my parents to let me play in the hotel pool before we headed out to a family event. They said I could as long as my older sister Julie went with me.

"Don't even *think* about going over there, Kristi! It's too deep, and you can't swim!" Julie shouted when she saw me eyeing the big green water slide at the deep end of the pool. I knew she was right, but the temptation to do what I wanted was too strong.

"I can handle it," I mumbled to myself as I jumped out of the little kid area, ran to the adult pool, and started to climb up the ladder before my sister could stop me. By the time I got to the top I realized that I may have been a little hasty. The slide was awfully high, and the water beneath looked *very* deep.

Maybe this wasn't such a good idea, I thought to myself. My intention was to head back down, but instead, one of my hands slipped off the railing and I fell face forward, belly down on the slide. Frantic, I grabbed at the edges in hopes of stopping myself. But I couldn't. It was too late.

Like a cannon ball, my body shot forward directly into the deepest part of the pool. Trying to scream for help, I took in a huge gulp of water, which made my chest burn as it went down my windpipe. My arms and legs flailed wildly as I tried to grab hold of anything that would keep my head above water, but nothing was there. I was drowning, and it was all my fault.

The third time I almost drowned I was twenty-three years old. By this time, I had no qualms about jumping into the warm ocean water in Mexico, since I now considered myself an excellent swimmer. Hours of lessons and years of swim time in our backyard pool had prepared me well. My two older sisters, Mindi and Shawn, had taken me to Cancun, Mexico, as a graduation gift. We'd spent most of the day swimming and jumping waves when a massive wave came out of nowhere and slammed me to the ocean floor. Before I could get my bearings, I was hit with another, then another. I thought I could swim my way back to shore but then the final wave hit me, pulling me right into the center of a riptide. I did everything I knew to do for as long as I could do it, but fatigue set in. I was too weary to fight anymore. With nothing left to give, I gave up. I was drowning.

As daunting as those near-drowning experiences were for me, the heart of each story revolves around the individuals who saved me. In each case a select few sacrificed a bit of themselves to care enough about my well-being to help me right where I was. They put their lives on pause to save my life. And the best part of all, they did what God desires each of us to do. They served me in my need with a heart of love.

They put the Word of God—his compassionate, redeeming, life-giving words—into action. And by their examples, they taught me one of the major keys to happiness. Sometimes it's not so much about seeking our own happiness as it is about learning how to seek the happiness of others!

What does it look like to seek the happiness of others? It's combining the power of speaking encouraging and Holy Spirit–driven words to others with the power of following up on those words to bring them to life. While words carry power within

SOMETIMES IT'S NOT

SO MUCH ABOUT

SEEKING OUR OWN

HAPPINESS AS IT IS

ABOUT LEARNING

HOW TO SEEK

THE HAPPINESS

OF OTHERS!

themselves, words are just words unless we combine them with action.

For example, if we tell someone all day, "I love you," but our actions don't reflect the meaning behind those words, then those words not only lose their meaning but also their power. In essence, we display our lack of belief in our own words, thus deflating their intended purpose and power.

It's a bit like what the apostle James talks about in James 2:15–16:

> Suppose a brother or a sister is without clothes and daily food. If one of you says to them, "Go in peace; keep warm and well fed," but does nothing about their physical needs, what good is it?

The key is to recognize that it's not only important what we say but also what we do to back up what we say.

The first time I almost drowned, it took me completely by surprise. What I remember the most vividly is seeing the familiar legs of people all around me, so close I could almost touch them, and realizing that despite their close proximity, my efforts to reach out for help were being ignored. In my fight to survive, I felt invisible. Hopeless.

But then my brother, who wasn't even in the pool at the time, recognized that I was in distress, ran to where I was, and jumped in to save me. Although there were plenty of people around who could have helped me, my brother was the only one who did. Why only him? Because he was the only one paying attention.

Often we become so consumed with our own lives that we fail to see the needs of others. Our lives revolve around ourselves, because our words are focused only on ourselves. Our conversations are peppered with words like *I* and *me* rather than *they* and *them*, or even *you*. This deafens us to others' cries for help, which only seems to magnify the lying words the enemy speaks over them.

Looking back on that first near-drowning experience, what I remember thinking over and over was, *How can they not see me drowning? How can they not hear my screams?*

How many times have we passed right by others asking those same questions, leading them to conclude, *Nobody cares for me, My life is not important*, or *God has forgotten me*? If we are to partner with God in demonstrating the love we profess to have for people, we must stop focusing only on ourselves and pay attention to one another's needs. This is how we give legs to our words and what we say we believe.

Sometimes, though, it seems as if maybe those who need help only have themselves to blame for their situations. We tell ourselves things like *They don't deserve my help* or *They made their bed so they have to lie in it*. Granted, there may be certain situations that warrant a posture of stepping back and allowing them to work it out on their own, but we have to be careful not to take on God's role, the only One who knows the heart and why people are in the situations they are in.

I would bet a million dollars that if we knew the backstory of people we are apt to dismiss and judge, we would not be so quick to withhold our love, encouragement, and service. My second near-drowning experience is a perfect example.

When I almost drowned in the hotel pool at six years old, it was my fault. I had defied my sister's rules, ignored her words of advice, and simply did what I wanted to do. She could have easily called for someone else to rescue me, especially considering her own unique set of circumstances, but she didn't. She took it upon herself to sacrifice her own needs for the sake of saving me.

I left out of the story that my sister was going to a special event that afternoon and had spent the entire morning getting ready, putting on her favorite outfit, and spending hours doing her hair. She was in no way prepared to jump into a pool, let alone mess up her hours of work in order to rescue her bratty little sister. Helping me was inconvenient, uncomfortable, and an act of selflessness, yet she did it.

Regardless of how wrong I was, Julie loved me enough to save me. She did what God calls us all to do: put words into action out of hearts of love, regardless of the foolishness of others.

My third near-drowning experience came when I just couldn't fight the waves anymore. I was in the water struggling for a long time before anyone realized that I was in serious trouble. While I tried to do everything I knew to do, it wasn't enough. And by the time my sisters recognized it, it was too late. They couldn't save me, so they had to call in the experts and let the lifeguards do their jobs.

This is probably the most common scenario for many of us. We actually see people in the deep end of life, but we tell ourselves that they are strong enough to handle it on their own. "They don't need our help," we say. "They can take care of themselves."

But they do need our help, and it's time for us to start doing something about it, whether it is going out of our way to speak encouragement and affirmation into their lives; quietly coming alongside them in the simple, everyday tasks to provide relief; offering our own skills as they apply to whatever situation they are in; or, even better, a combination of all those things. Although a person might seem to be a "spiritual giant" in our eyes, no one can live this life on their own.

We *all* need help at times. We *all* need people to lift us up with loving hearts. And we *all* need someone to talk *us* happy when we're too weary, tired, and beaten down to do it on our own. The key to true happiness is the ability to give the gift of happiness to others by seeing them, loving them, encouraging them, and putting our words into action.

———

"Come on, girl, let's get this done," Kursti said in her strong Georgia drawl.

From the moment I met Kursti Woolard she was a force to be reckoned with. Even though we were strangers at our first meeting, it was as though we had known each other our entire lives. "It was a God setup," we say jokingly.

Kursti was a direct answer to my prayers. She was exactly what I needed when I needed it. I had no clue where to begin when it came to running my own company, but Kursti did. She is a financial advisor and a top-notch business woman. But what makes her so cool is that while she has a great business mind, she also has an incredible heart for God.

THE KEY TO TRUE
HAPPINESS IS THE
ABILITY TO GIVE THE
GIFT OF HAPPINESS
TO OTHERS BY SEEING
THEM, LOVING THEM,
ENCOURAGING THEM,
AND PUTTING OUR
WORDS INTO ACTION.

Everything she does is a direct result of her love for God. She is the perfect example of someone who puts the Word of God into action by encouraging and serving others with a heart of love. She has learned the art of talking others happy.

"We can do this! And whatever we don't know how to do, God will show us."

Even though I was a nervous wreck thinking about all the elements it would take to start this new adventure, Kursti wasn't fazed one bit. Whether it was over the phone or while sitting at my kitchen table with a laptop and stacks of paper, Kursti was always talking me happy.

"Girl, we can get this done in no time. Look, I'll show you how to build your website. I'll help you file all the right paperwork to start your own business, and I'll help you get things in order for you to establish your own 501c3. We can do this, girl! And it's going to be *good*!"

I had no clue that a 501c3 was a nonprofit; I thought it was a math equation. But regardless of my less-than-smart moments, Kursti laughed it off with me and walked me through it all, teaching me along the way. Her words of encouragement didn't carry empty promises; rather, she fulfilled them, put them into action, and brought life to my heart.

Once I got past my own hang-ups, the process of walking in the new became really fun and rewarding. We both put God's promises into action by trusting his Word over our lives. We called on God every step of the way and expected nothing less than excellence from him. And that's what he always gave us. It was amazing, and it thrilled us both and it made us happy.

Kursti's words to me didn't just spark a renewed sense of hope in my heart; her words watered the seeds within and chipped away at the walls of limitations I had placed around myself.

"Girl, you're more than just television. God has given you so many gifts. You have a heart for the Lord, Kristi. It's time to use what God has given you to bless the world. Let's get it done!"

All the things I had previously told myself I couldn't do, Kursti had me doing. Never in my wildest dreams would I have imagined that I could start my own production company or build my own website or establish a nonprofit to help women. I had no clue! But the Lord used Kursti to build me up, to challenge me, and to put my faith in him into action.

All those lies I had told myself or allowed others to speak to me, such as "I'm not good enough or smart enough or talented enough," or lies such as "I can't do it," or "I can't handle it," were all words that contradicted the truth of God's Word. God used Kursti, as well as several others, to speak truth into my life. And in doing so, they did what God wants us all to do: talk others happy.

STEPS TO TALK OTHERS HAPPY

As important as it is for us to talk ourselves happy, it's just as important to learn how to talk others happy. We can do that when we remind ourselves to open our eyes to the needs around us. Following are some questions to consider as we pursue this change in our daily focus.

- *Who can you help today?* Look around, and choose to see someone who is struggling right in front of you. Ask God to show you what you can do for that person. Or, better yet, go to the person directly and ask how you can help.
- *Whose needs have you overlooked because you've quietly judged them in their circumstances?* Ask God to help you examine your heart regarding people you've had the ability to help but chose not to out of judgment. Ask God to forgive you and to give you the right perspective regarding these individuals.

NOW TAKE IT, SPEAK IT, AND LIVE IT!

1. Read Galatians 6:2 and John 15:13 out loud. Write one of them down on a sticky note, and read it aloud to yourself throughout the day as a reminder of what it is to walk in God's love.

2. Get together with a few friends and prayerfully consider who in your community may be in need of encouragement or help. Formulate a plan leaning on one another's talents to reach out to this person not only with words of support and truth but also with actions that back up those words.

8

promise

The Purpose Is in the Promise

I knew I had one too many books piled up in my arms, but I didn't want to make another trip downstairs. As I reached for my office door, the books began to slide and topple over. I quickly shifted my body to catch them from falling, and out of the corner of my eye I saw a little yellow sticky note fall out from between one of the pages.

Initially, I planned to disregard the note, but then I noticed something scribbled in red. Curious, I squatted down, balanced the top of the books with my chin, and swooped up the note. When I read the words, I froze.

The note had been written exactly a year before. I had been in a really dark place and couldn't figure out why God seemed to have simply shut me out. My life had been at a standstill, and I wasn't sure if I had failed God or God had failed me. My heart had been burdened, my soul weary, and by all accounts, I had lost hope.

"I just want to be happy," I had said time and time again not fully realizing what that really meant. With time, however, the Lord revealed to me that it wasn't mere happiness I was searching for—I longed to be fulfilled.

"New Job. New House. New Husband. New Life," the little yellow sticky note read. I had believed with all my heart that these things would give me everything I needed to feel whole again. They became my focus and my pursuit.

My prayers fixated on them.

My mind was consumed by them.

And my words idolized them.

The *new* in the form of a job, home, spouse, and life became my hope.

I had stashed several notes like that around the house, as if they would come to pass simply through osmosis.

"*If* I get a new job, *then* I'll be happy."

"*If* I get a new house, *then* I'll be happy."

"*If* I get a new husband, *then* I'll be happy."

And, for good measure, "*If* I lose this extra weight, *then* I'll be happy."

Reading these notes had not only given me hope but also a sense of expectancy and belief that my life would be better as soon as I obtained those things. After all, I only wanted what everybody else already had.

I was tired of being alone and having to take on life as a single parent.

I wanted a job where people appreciated me and didn't just tolerate me.

And I wanted to live some place new that didn't carry so

many memories and have so many faces looking in on my life as spectators rather than helpful participants.

I had grown tired of the old, and I wanted something new to hope for: new opportunities, new possibilities, new relationships—just, *new*.

I stacked the books beside me as I sat quietly on the floor considering the past year. Slowly, I began crumpling up the note in my hand. Even though I had written those words a year before, the desire for those things had been in my heart for a very long time.

As time passed, though, I found I could no longer speak with a level of certainty that what I once hoped for, even longed for, were God's will and promises for my life. So, I stopped talking about them in the hopes that I would stop thinking about them. And maybe if I stopped thinking about them, then I could release my grip of hope for them.

I didn't realize at the time that the Lord didn't necessarily want me to change what I was hoping for as much as change how I viewed what I was hoping for. God was teaching me that the fulfillment of my dreams couldn't be the source of my happiness; rather, it had to be God's presence, power, and active participation in my life.

For instance, technically, I still didn't have all the things on that little yellow sticky note, but in a it-makes-no-kind-of-sense way, I did.

No, I didn't have that traditional job or what some would call a "hot-shot" career any longer, but God gave me the tools to start my own production company, as well as a vision for a ministry.

No, I didn't have a new house in which to escape the old

memories. But God did provide me with ways to make my house new, including opportunities to create new and special memories. And no, I didn't have the fine-looking, tall, brilliant, rich new husband—*yet*, but God had clearly stepped in and taken care of me and Chase as a husband would.

The truth was that I felt more fulfilled in my life than I ever had before—emotionally, mentally, and definitely spiritually.

The joy in my heart.
The peace in my mind.
And the rest in my soul.

Knowing I could trust that God was right there with me—in front of me, behind me, and all around me—filled my heart with joy. I was grateful for all the ways the Lord had helped me in this past season. And, I was learning that God's handprint on my life was more valuable than any new job, home, or husband.

I was just about to get up and throw away the little yellow sticky note when I felt the Lord speak to my heart. "Kristi, those promises are still for you. I wanted to show you that while each will bless you and even give you a sense of happiness, what I desire to give you is what your heart truly longs for."

Then, as if God turned on a light within my heart, I got it! God changed my perspective about each of those promises, and suddenly everything became crystal clear! It wasn't that I needed those *things* to be happy; however, *I did need what each of those things represented to be happy.*

IT WASN'T
THAT I NEEDED
THOSE *THINGS*
TO BE HAPPY;
HOWEVER, *I DID*
NEED WHAT EACH
OF THOSE THINGS
REPRESENTED
TO BE HAPPY.

New job.

New house.

New husband.

New life.

My desire for a new job was really my heart longing *to know my purpose in life*, my identity and my significance in this world. I wanted to know why God created me and what he created me for. The Lord revealed my purpose through his Word and re-established my identity by the power of the Holy Spirt working through me and in me to create a new me.

My desire for a new house was really my heart longing to *know that God would provide for me, take care of me, and protect me*. The Lord did all the above with a unique set of circumstances. He provided a steady source of income from a place I never would have imagined while he also opened up incredible doors of opportunities that allowed me to use the gifts he created in me.

My desire for a new husband was really my heart longing to *know that I was loved unconditionally* even when I made the worst mistakes. It pointed to a desire to know that someone loved me enough to think of me, care for me, and assure me that no matter how difficult life became, their love would never abandon me, fail me, betray me, or reject me. God did that for me. Even when I questioned him, got angry with him, and downright disobeyed him, his love for me never wavered. In fact, when I believed I was the most unlovable, he poured out his love that much more on me.

My desire for a new life was really my heart longing for God to *make me new*. God did that as he taught me to see others as he sees them. And to see myself as he sees me. He silenced the words of the world that told me I was never good enough, smart enough, thin enough, pretty enough, rich enough, or successful enough. In changing my perspective, he transformed my heart into the reflection of his heart; he made me new.

While I was thankful for how the Lord met my spiritual needs and changed my perspective toward those things I had once sought to find hope in, I still longed for the physical representation of them. Especially the husband. I wanted to be married again. And not just married for the sake of being married; I desired to have someone to share my life with and partner with. But I wasn't so sure if my desire was just a desire or an actual promise from God.

As I sat on the floor in my office staring at the crumpled-up yellow sticky note, it was as if I could hear that quiet voice saying, "Kristi, the promise is *still* for you."

Is it? I wondered, wanting to hope again. *It's not too late?*

God's promises are for each and every one of his children. And his promises are broader and go much deeper than what many of us fully understand. We are spiritual and physical beings, which means that we need to be fed in both areas of our lives to be fulfilled. As a result, God's promises to us, through his Word, are meant to fulfill the totality of us.

For instance, there are certain promises in the Bible that attend to the inner-man, or rather the spirit-man. Promises such as those that tell us God will heal the broken areas of our hearts

(Psalm 147:3) or promises that God will never lie to us (Numbers 23:19). We all need promises like those so we can have an assurance within our hearts and a comfort within our minds that God's Word and love for us is true, active, and unceasing.

On the other hand, there are promises God gives that are specific to our physical needs, such as God's promise to the Israelites in Deuteronomy 7:15: "The LORD will keep you free from every disease. He will not inflict on you the horrible diseases you knew in Egypt."

The difference between the two kinds of promises is that the spiritual promises *fulfill* us as they are targeted to meet the needs within our hearts, whereas the physical promises *bless* us as they are targeted to meet the physical needs of our bodies. Both are equally important, because God uses them to make us complete and whole in him!

But what about the third kind of promise? You know, that secret promise that God has given just to you simply because he loves you. The kind of promise that he plants within the depths of your heart, and no matter what you do, the longing for it never ceases until you see its fulfillment.

The promise of a husband is that special promise for me. My challenge, however, is that as I continue to witness the passing of time without seeing it come to pass, I'm often tempted to speak words that contradict the very thing I'm hoping and waiting for. Words such as, "Maybe I missed it" or "Maybe it's too late," or "Maybe that's not God's plan for my life anymore."

But we have to fight by speaking words that come into agreement with what God promised us so that we can continue to have hope in it and faith in God for it. Words are power. Our words are not the only words, however, that have impact on our lives. Often, the words of those around us carry an even greater level of influence on our lives and on how we perceive the possibility of that promise.

I can't tell you how many times my spirit has been crushed by the negative words of someone I care for who used their words to contradict God's promises for me. In the case of my husband, people have spoken words such as "You're better off without a husband," "You don't really want one," and "They are no good." Maybe their words were intended to protect me or even warn me, but the truth is that their negative words always discouraged me and, at times, made me question if God's promise was the best thing for me.

When fear or doubts come upon us, sparked by words spoken to us, we have to fight back with the truth of the Word. Especially the Word that reminds us of God's character. He's a good God who loves us more than we can possibly imagine. And when God promises to give us something, that something is good.

The key is using our own words to keep hope alive. Our words breathe life into a situation by keeping that which God has spoken at the forefront of our thoughts, hearts, and speech. When negative words are thrown in the mix we have to shut them up and shut them down. We can no longer allow anyone else or even ourselves to crush our spirits by saying things such as "It's never going to happen" or "It's too late for it to happen."

We must choose to use our words as igniters of hope by saying things like "*When* it happens . . ." or even "I *know* it's going to happen." When we do that, it keeps the fire of hope for that promise alive and builds a feeling of happiness in anticipation for what is to come!

We can hope all day long, but sometimes our greatest enemy is the clock. We can have an assurance in our hearts that God is going to do what he promised to do, but if we're not careful, we will allow the anxiety that often comes with the passing of time to steal every ounce of our joy, hope, and happiness in the process of the wait.

One of the greatest illustrations of this challenge is found in the Bible in the story of Sarah and Abraham. Here's my modern-day interpretation of their story found in the book of Genesis, chapters 15, 16, 17, and 18:

Sarah had everything. She was drop-dead gorgeous, had a madly rich husband and a staff of servants who gave her everything she could ever imagine. Everything, except for the *one* thing she desperately wanted more than anything else. The absence of that one thing was the reason why Sarah was so unhappy.

For years and years, she hoped, she prayed, and she believed, but all efforts on her part seemed to fail. God had given Sarah and her husband a promise, and that promise was a child. But month after month after month, Sarah peed on a stick as they waited and hoped, then fought back the tears of disappointment—only to experience it all over again.

After ten long years of nothing, Sarah and her husband took it upon themselves to do something. By now the Word of God seemed faint compared to the intensity of their own words, which carried doubts such as, "Maybe we heard God wrong" and "Maybe

God meant for our child to come to us in a different way." They started to trust in what they saw rather than in what God said.

So they did what many of us do: they played Holy Ghost Junior and tried to take matters into their own hands. Sarah suggested that Abraham sleep with one of her servants to conceive a child on Sarah's behalf, kind of like a surrogate.

He did.

She did.

And it happened.

But it didn't turn out as they had hoped.

Not only did this decision not bring Sarah and her husband the happiness they desired, but their disobedience and lack of trust that God would fulfill the promise in his way and in his time resulted in monumental negative consequences that have lasted to this day.

Thirteen years later, and still nothing. God came to them *again* and reiterated the promise that they would have a child out of Sarah's womb. But she couldn't take it anymore. The first time God had spoken the promise to her husband it had been twenty-three, twenty-four years before. The promise that once carried such hope now felt like God taunting them with the impossible. God's word sounded absurd.

Even if Sarah wasn't so obviously infertile, she couldn't have a child now, because, well, she was old. And not like just-got-on-Social-Security kind of old. She was the kind of old that warranted an honorable mention in the Guinness Book of World Records. Abraham was one hundred years old, and Sarah was, well, not too far off from that.

It is a twisted joke, she thought when she overheard some men of God reiterate the promise to her husband—again. *Whatever. I'm over it,* she said within her heart, discarding every word spoken about the promise she no longer believed. So, she laughed. But her laughter was only to keep herself from crying.

God knows that at times our faith can soar to the mountaintops, yet moments later something can be said or done that plunges our faith into deep valleys of doubt and discouragement. But even still, God's love for us and the purpose for which he created us will be fulfilled as we continue to believe in that special promise he's given us.

God is patient, and he compassionately understands every one of our frailties, yet never holds them against us. In fact, it's our frailties that drive us into complete dependence on the Almighty God.

The first time God spoke to Abraham about the promise of a child, Abraham was seventy-five years old. Ten years later, Abraham and Sarah decided to take matters into their own hands by attempting to force the promise into existence. Abraham slept with Hagar, Sarah's maidservant, and she conceived a child named Ishmael. But that wasn't the promise God had for them.

Then, more than thirteen years later, God came to Abraham again to reaffirm the promise. This time, God laid out some important things they needed to remember, takeaways we all must use to encourage us in order to adjust our words and our ways of thinking to regain hope.

Let's take a look at the biblical account and begin with Genesis 17:

When Abram was ninety-nine years old, the LORD appeared to him and said, "*I am God Almighty; walk before me faithfully and be blameless. Then I will make my covenant between me and you* and will greatly increase your numbers."

Abram fell facedown, and God said to him, "As for me, this is my covenant with you: *You will be the father of many nations.* No longer will you be called Abram; *your name will be Abraham, for I have made you a father of many nations.* (vv. 1–5)

- Here's the key: encourage yourself in the wait by telling yourself what God can do!

  "*I am God Almighty!*" Even before God spoke about the promise again, God reminded Abraham who he is. "I am God Almighty." Meaning, God can do anything, and his might is greater than our frailties, insecurities, and inabilities. The Hebrew word for God is *El Shaddai*, which emphasizes God's might and power. God is a God of the impossible. So whatever he said, he will do—no matter what! The key is in telling ourselves that the promise isn't contingent upon who *we* are but *who God is*!

- Encourage yourself by telling yourself that just as *you* are special to God so is his promise to you!

  "*Then I will make my covenant between me and you.*" Your promise is *your* promise.

  Some promises are universal; God commits to them

for all of us no matter what. For example, "I will never leave you or forsake you" is a promise we can all count on.

Some promises are contingent upon our own actions, such as "*if* you confess with your mouth and believe in your heart, *then* you will be saved."

And some promises are specific to the individual. This was the case for Abraham and Sarah. God's promise to Abraham that he would be the father of many nations was specifically for him. Strange, considering the fact that his wife couldn't have children. But the limitations we see in ourselves never thwart the purposes that God has for our lives.

In fact, I'm convinced God loves the challenges, because when he does what he says he's going to do, no one will be able to take the credit or get the glory other than the One who fulfilled it. God Almighty.

• Encourage yourself by speaking life into the promise as if you already have it.

"No longer will you be called Abram; *your name will be Abraham, for I have made you a father of many nations.*" Abram means "High Father" or "Patriarch," and Abraham means "Father of a Multitude." This is a perfect example of God showing us the power in what we call ourselves. God changed Abraham's name so that his name would reflect *who God was calling him to be.* A father! And not just a father to one, but a father to a multitude that included nations, kings, and leaders of the world. What a promise!

I love this part of the commentary in my Bible:

Let God's words, which designated His will and promise for your life, become as fixed in your mind and as
governing of your speech as God's changing Abraham's
name was in shaping his concept of himself. Do not
name yourself anything less than God does. (*The New
Spirit Filled Life Bible*, NKJV, p. 26)

God was showing Abraham—and, in turn, us—that
what we call ourselves is what we think of ourselves.
Abraham was calling himself a father of nations even
though the promise was not yet realized and he certainly
didn't look that way yet. But looks don't matter in God's
realm. We don't see as God sees. That's where our faith
comes into play.

If God promised to heal you, say, "I am healed!"

If God promised to restore your marriage, say, "God
has saved our marriage."

To the world it sounds insane, but so does the premise of a one-hundred-year-old man and a ninety-year-old
woman having a baby! It's up to us to keep that promise at
the forefront of our speech.

Skip down to chapter 17, verses 15–16:

God also said to Abraham, "As for Sarai your wife, you
are no longer to call her Sarai; her name will be Sarah. I
will bless her and will surely give you a son by her. I will
bless her so that she will be the *mother* of nations; kings
of peoples will come from her."

- Encourage yourself by believing you are who God says you are!

   "As for Sarai your wife, you are no longer to call her Sarai; her name will be Sarah." Sarai means "princess." Sarah means *"the* princess" or *"the* queen." At first, I didn't fully understand the name change or grasp the significance. Then it dawned on me. The word *the* in front of princess and *the* in front of queen was God emphasizing Sarah's value, her significance, her role, and her worth.

   During those days, being able to have a child was a pretty big deal. It defined your worth, value, and even your womanhood. I can only imagine how miserable Sarah felt about her situation. She probably struggled with a negative self-image.

   As with many of us women, when society or culture tells us that we've fallen short in some area of our lives, it's easy to tell ourselves that we're broken, less than, or even not enough. But God was reminding Sarah and others of her worth, significance, and value every time her name was spoken! Her significance wasn't in whether or not she could bear a child, although that was the promise. She was significant and important because that's what God said she was! As with Abraham, God was getting Sarah to see herself as God saw her through the power of her own spoken name.

   So many of us get tripped up by what we're not or what we can't do that we fall into the bad habit of defining ourselves by our perceived limitations. But that is not how

God sees us, nor is it how God determines our value in this world.

God picked a woman who physically could not have a child to be the one who would carry the child of promise. I love that! Because that alone reminds us that it's *all* God. What he wants to do. Who he wants us to be. How he chooses to see us. It's all on him. We just have to learn how to come into agreement with him with our words and with our beliefs about ourselves.

- Encourage others to speak of you as God speaks of you. In other words, shut down and shut up the naysayers.

God said to Abraham, "As for Sarai your wife, *you are no longer to call her Sarai; her name will be Sarah.*" Here God is showing us the importance and the power in what we call each other. Yes, it was important for Sarah to know her value and worth based upon what God called her, but it was just as important for those who had the power to speak into her life to recognize her value and worth by aligning their words with God's words.

Our words have impact not just on ourselves and on our lives but on the lives of others. Are we calling the people around us what God says to call them, or are we referring to them as we see them? We must remember that we have the power to build each other up or to tear each other down, and God wants us to choose the former. After all, God doesn't see us as others see us—as in everything that's wrong with us. God sees us through the reflection of his Son, Jesus. Praise God for that!

Let's keep reading through Genesis 17:17 and Genesis 18:10–12:

> Abraham fell facedown; he laughed and said to himself, "Will a son be born to a man a hundred years old? Will Sarah bear a child at the age of ninety?"
> Now Sarah was listening at the entrance to the tent, which was behind him. Abraham and Sarah were already very old, and Sarah was past the age of child-bearing. So Sarah laughed to herself as she thought, "After I am worn out and my lord is old, will I now have this pleasure?"

Do you ever wonder why it's easier to tell ourselves why things *can't* happen than why they *can* happen? Let's face it, some things are just easier to believe than others. Especially when they fit into human reason. But when God says he'll do something completely out of the realm of feasibility, it's difficult to fight the feeling of doubt and disbelief. Especially when time is a factor. As in, time keeps ticking, but the promise seems to be fleeting.

Abraham and Sarah felt that way. They both laughed when God came back to them after two decades to affirm his promise. Remember, Abraham was almost one hundred years old, and Sarah was knocking on ninety.

No matter how impossible we tell ourselves a situation is, though, God can handle it. God loves a challenge. He loves to prove his faithfulness to us. Not for his sake, but for our sakes.

In fact, in spite of Sarah's and Abraham's reactions, and in spite of the many ways they disqualified themselves from being able to receive the promise, and in spite of the ways they told themselves and each other how incapable they were of being able to fulfill the promise, God got right in front of their excuses and slapped them with the truth of his own Word. He asked, "Is anything too hard for the LORD?" (Genesis 18:14). *No!* And how do we know that? Because of who God is.

God Almighty.

The God of might.

The God of the impossible!

When all physical signs point away from the promises of God, we have to speak words of faith and not words of fear based on what we see.

If God promised to heal you, he will heal you!

If God promised to send you a spouse, he will send you a spouse. And a good one! (That's what I tell myself.)

And if God promised to take care of you with a job or finances or whatever, God will do it!

It makes us sad or discouraged when the words of how we feel become louder than the words of what we know God will do.

Just like Abraham, we have to remind ourselves of the promise by keeping it at the forefront of our minds. And just like Sarah, we have to make sure that we, as well as others, are speaking words that line up with the value, worth, and significance that God has placed upon us.

What happens after all that? Let's take a look at Genesis 21:

WHEN ALL PHYSICAL
SIGNS POINT AWAY
FROM THE PROMISES
OF GOD, WE HAVE
TO SPEAK WORDS
OF FAITH AND
NOT WORDS OF
FEAR BASED ON
WHAT WE SEE.

And the LORD visited Sarah as He had said, and the LORD did for Sarah as *He had spoken.* For Sarah conceived and bore Abraham a son in his old age, at the set time of which God had *spoken to him.* And Abraham called the name of his son who was born to him—whom Sarah bore to him—Isaac. . . . And Sarah said, "God has made me laugh, and all who hear will laugh with me." (vv. 1–3, 6 NKJV)

Their son's name meant "laughter," so every time they spoke his name, they reminded themselves of how God had turned their laughter laced with pain into a laughter filled with his joy. A joy not only brought about by God's fulfilled promise but also by the faith they had in God.

When God speaks, it's as good as done. No matter how long it takes. His Word is power, and his promises will be fulfilled. That's why we have to remind ourselves that God's promises to us don't depend upon our behavior but rather on his faithfulness!

We could save ourselves a lot of emotional turmoil and heartache if we would just stop fighting in the realm of the physical—meaning, fighting against the obstacles of what we see or don't see—and instead started fighting in the realm of the spiritual by speaking what God sees. That's what makes us happy.

Happiness is not only in the fulfillment of the promise; happiness is cultivated in the confirming of God's Word within our hearts, minds, and words.

Growing our faith is actually more important to God than finally obtaining his promises for us. Why? Because it's our faith that pleases God and shows him that we trust him. It's our faith that eventually leads us into God's purposes for our lives. God's purpose for Abraham was to become the father of a nation. A nation of people who would declare the God of Abraham their God and produce generations of faithful servants to the Lord.

And it all began with the promised son whose name meant laughter. After all, our faith in God is the root from which our happiness grows.

———

As I stood up from the floor and walked over to my desk, I placed the yellow sticky note right in front of me. Slowly, yet deliberately, I uncrumpled the note and smoothed it out with my hand. This time, when I read the words on the note I read them out loud.

"New Job. New House. New Husband. New Life." But this time I chose to fuel the fire of hope with my words as I continued by saying, "Thank you, Lord, for your promises to me. And thank you for what you've done and what you're doing. After all, since you said it, I *know* you will do it!"

STEPS TO TALK YOURSELF HAPPY

God loves to give his children promises that we can hold on to, be expectant about, and grow our faith through. As important as God's wonderful promises are for our lives, however, God uses the process of waiting for the promise to unveil his

HAPPINESS IS
NOT ONLY IN THE
FULFILLMENT OF THE
PROMISE; HAPPINESS
IS CULTIVATED IN
THE CONFIRMING
OF GOD'S WORD
WITHIN OUR HEARTS,
MINDS, AND WORDS.

purpose. As you work to reorient your perspective, here are a few questions to consider:

- *What is the purpose God wants you to learn as you wait for your special promises?* It is in the purpose where we see God working in us from the inside out, transforming areas of our hearts and character to better to reflect his. Maybe God is teaching you how to have patience or peace. Take a moment to consider the lessons he has already taught you and the ones you are in the process of learning.
- *What promise are you waiting for?* Search your heart to pin down a few concrete promises that the Lord has given you, and hold on to them tightly. Breathe life back into them as you speak about them and watch God unveil them before your eyes.

NOW TAKE IT, SPEAK IT, AND LIVE IT!

1. Get a yellow sticky note. Write down these words to remind yourself: "Is anything too hard for the Lord?"
2. Read through the story of Abraham and Sarah beginning in Genesis 15, and encourage yourself by remembering that God has a set time for everything.
3. Join together with one or two of your trusted friends. Begin by sharing your special promises with each other. Then, think of ways each of you can prepare yourself

for the *when*. Don't forget to use your words to agree with that promise by saying things such as "When it happens" and "I know it will happen." Before long, you'll find the joy in the process as much as in the fulfillment of the promise!

Conclusion

How to Talk Yourself Happy

He shifted his body to lean in closer. His face was within inches of my face, and his eyes were searing into mine when he said . . .

"I'm *smarter* than you.

I'm *wiser* than you.

I'm *more spiritual* than you.

I *know more* than you.

I have the right to talk, and *you don't!*"

His words hung in the air as if waiting for me to grab hold of them. But I didn't. Because in that moment I realized the power I had within me. That power must have been a force to be reckoned with if the enemy was doing everything in his power to shut me up and shut me down.

That's who I was standing up against. *The enemy.* Sure, he was using a man I knew to deliver those belittling words, but I was well aware of the source behind them. He had tried on many occasions to tear me down and render me powerless with words similar to these, and for far too long I had allowed the enemy to succeed, to pierce a hole in my heart and drain every drop of joy the Lord had filled me with.

I had tried to fill that hole with other things and had allowed those lying words to seize my happiness, but in that moment I had had enough. I pulled my back up straight and said, "God has done some amazing things in my life. And I would like to share them. I *will* share them, because I *do* have a right to talk!"

I didn't realize it at the time, but this was the beginning of God teaching me how to talk myself happy. I told myself that I was not going to be silenced anymore. I decided I was taking back my power, my happy, and I was going to do so by choosing the ultimate weapon: the Word!

I started digging into what God has to say about happiness. I realized that our happiness isn't contingent on exterior factors in the form of things or people. Rather, true happiness is birthed from within our hearts!

A good man brings good things out of the good stored
up in his heart, and an evil man brings evil things out
of the evil stored up in his heart. *For the mouth speaks
what the heart is full of.* (Luke 6:45)

The process of talking yourself happy is as much about the condition of our hearts as it is about the quality of our words. As the above passage says, "For the mouth speaks what the heart is full of." If our words are a reflection of our hearts, we must not only change our words but, more important, we must allow God to transform our hearts. This happens when we allow the power of the Holy Spirit to preside over our lives and we immerse ourselves in the love of God by abiding in the Word of God.

This process of integrating biblical principles into every aspect of our lives acts as a cleaning agent to rid our hearts of all the debris that has accumulated over the years. God's Word not only cleanses us, but it also fills us back up.

Scripture says, *"A good man brings good things out of the good stored up in his heart."* That *"good"* comes by way of planting the seed of God's Word, watering that Word by our faith, and speaking that Word forth to create growth.

Key principles such as compassion, trust, forgiveness, and obedience, just to name a few, can act as a form of fertilizer that promotes exceptional growth toward the "good things." And it's in that place of *good* within our hearts that we'll not only find happiness and joy but also the seeds of God's promises for us personally.

The most phenomenal thing about having a relationship with Jesus Christ is that God is such a personal God. He knows every one of our hearts and places specific promises within them just for us. And if God has placed them there, then he will fulfill them.

I can think of a small handful of those special personal promises God has given me through the years. Some God has already fulfilled, while others I'm still waiting for. God not only gives us those promises to bless us with an abundant life, but he uses those promises to build our faith in him. And it's our faith in God that pleases him and makes him happy.

On the flip side, if our faith—our reliance, trust, and dependency on God—makes God happy, and us happy in return, then we know that it's our faith that makes the enemy angry. So what does the enemy do about it? He tries to take us down by sabotaging our faith and derailing us from the promises of God.

The enemy doesn't want us to be blessed or to have a heart of love for the things of God. He wants to do everything he can to fill our hearts up with the weight of the world so that there is no room left for the joy, peace, and hope that God desires for us.

We have to remind ourselves that the enemy's goal is to steal, kill, and destroy every good thing God has for those he loves. He wants to *steal* our promises by *killing* our faith while attempting to *destroy* our hope with the use of negative, hurtful, and lying words. But God has given us the wisdom and the way to fight back. And that's with the *Word*!

When we are hit with the attacks of the enemy, we have to remind ourselves that he doesn't have reign over our lives or our promises. He can't touch them or take them away, because they are God's gifts to us. We have to speak the Word of Truth out loud so that we can literally drown out the negative voices in our minds. And we have to speak forth what we don't yet see but what we *know* in our hearts.

That *knowing* is what negates the lies of the enemy. The enemy targets the issues of the heart, because that's where our promises are held. This is why we must allow the peace of God to guard our hearts and minds in Christ Jesus (Philippians 4) and remember that if God spoke it, we can count it as done.

———

I was on assignment with *The 700 Club* many years ago to produce a story. I had to travel to Montclair, New Jersey, to attend Christ Church with Pastor David Ireland to interview him. I had briefly met with him that Saturday for a quick interview, then attended the Sunday morning service to shoot some extra footage. It was October 21, and on this particular Sunday, Pastor Ireland was teaching on God's promises. Just before he closed out the service he had the congregation stand up and pray.

"Place in your heart a promise that the Lord has given to you. Because he's going to do that for you. Just put it right there," he said.

Immediately, two promises came to mind. One was my son, who wasn't even a twinkle in my eye yet at the time, and the other was a promise relating to my heart's desire for a job in television. I began to pray, or, rather, speak to God about these two promises. I went back and forth between them, unsure which one to ask for or believe in. If God gave me the one, could I also hope for the other?

Just then, the pastor responded to my heart's cry. Out of hundreds of strangers in the middle of a church I had never stepped foot in before, he called me out.

"Yes, Kristi, you can."

Then he said, "Step forward, please."

I almost peed in my pants from the shock that God would use a complete stranger to call me by name and answer the prayer I had spoken silently within the depths of my heart.

"For I have called you to be a voice of hope. A voice to liberate those who are in adversity and those who are in pain . . ."

I stood at the front of that church completely overwhelmed by the words God was speaking through his servant. I couldn't believe that God loved me so much that he would speak directly to me in such a profound way. That moment impacted my faith walk tremendously.

That was the day I realized God hears our prayers and speaks to us. He actually speaks! Now, granted, he used a pastor from New Jersey, but nevertheless, God was speaking. And he was telling me that he was going to fulfill his promise by using me to speak too!

"For I have called you to be a *voice* of hope . . ."

That phrase *voice of hope* rang through my heart and played over and over in my mind. That had been my heart's desire from the time I was a child, and now God was speaking it out loud as if to activate it. Pastor David Ireland's words did just that. They activated my faith to hold on to a promise that the Lord had given just for me.

While God has used me to be a voice of hope and encouragement through a variety of means such as television, speaking engagements, and now through books, I'm still waiting for the full manifestation of that specific promise he gave just to me. I know that it's any day now. It's so close that I can see it and sense its nearness, especially since God has used the challenges in my life to test me, teach me, and transform my heart into the reflection of God. For years I wondered why it was taking so long. I thought that if I just prayed harder or believed more, then it would make the promise come quicker. At times I even told myself that I missed out on the promise because God no longer felt that I was worthy to receive it.

Other times I told myself that my mistakes—sins— disqualified me from the promise. And for far too long I allowed the critical words of others to make me believe that I was incapable of walking out the promise. But, praise God, I've since learned the truth.

The truth is that when God makes a promise to us, he will fulfill it.

The truth is that God considers the process just as important as obtaining the promise.

And the truth is that it takes seasons of challenge to purge things from our hearts so that God can make room for the promise.

God says to take delight in him and he will give us the desires of our hearts, so he wants our hearts to be filled with the good . . . and if that means using trials and tribulations to trim off all the hindering agents within our hearts, then so be it. God will get the glory, and we will, in turn, experience his gladness.

The key is to stop listening to the lies of the enemy and repeating them to ourselves. All the enemy is capable of doing is lying, so we need to learn how to shut him down. When he tries to tell us that the delayed promise is our fault or that God is withholding it from us or punishing us, we have to tell him what we know to be true from the Word of God and stand firm in that knowing—regardless of what we see or don't see.

A part of my promise states that God will use me to be "a voice of hope." A *voice*. It wasn't until that very moment when I was sitting across from the man telling me I didn't have the right to speak that I realized what the enemy was trying to do during my season of challenge. He was trying to get me so distracted and discouraged by my circumstances that I would simply forget or even forfeit what God was calling me to do. He was trying to speak against my destiny.

And for a moment, a single moment, I almost allowed him to.

The enemy was using this willing vessel to silence my *voice*. Because if he silenced my voice, then he could prevent God from using me to speak words of hope, healing, and encouragement to his children. He was trying to silence the "happy." But the enemy failed.

Instead of succeeding in derailing me and stealing what was left of my hope and joy, his bitter words opened my eyes. And God showed me and taught me that I am the one with the power, because I have his Word.

And as long as we have the Word—as in *the* Word *of* God, the Word who *is* God, and the Word that proceeds out of our mouths as we hold on to the promises of God—then *we will always be able to triumph over the enemy.*

We will always be able to walk in faith, live with hope, and talk ourselves happy!

STEPS TO TALK YOURSELF HAPPY

- *Remember the past and what the Lord has done in your life.* Speak often of God's faithfulness. Tell yourself and others about the ways God has helped in the little things, the hidden places, and the not-so-obvious moments of your life. If he did it before, he'll do it again.
- *Recognize who God is*—the character of God and the

heart and ways of God. Remind yourself and others that God does not lie, that he is all-knowing, all-powerful, and sovereign and has your best in mind.

- *Recite the Word of God and his specific promises for you,* agreeing with them in your speech but also in your heart. Allow the Word to bring light into your situation.
- *Realize the power of the Holy Spirit and surrender yourself to his will by humbly choosing to depend solely on his wisdom, his counsel, his help, his love, his power, and his instruction.* Allow this surrender to be reflected in your prayers.
- *Readjust your perspective to line up with God's.* As you speak God's Word, make sure you are not trying to manipulate it to line up with your lifestyle and your ways. Study it and speak it in its fullness.
- *Reach out to and connect with others who share the heart of God and can stand in agreement with the promises you are holding on to.* Encourage them in the Word just as you encourage yourself.
- *Relish in the goodness of God by praising him* and simply being thankful for the hope that *was* and *is* and *is to come* in our Abba Father, Jesus Christ.

Acknowledgments

Lord God, only you knew what was in store for me in this crazy season. What amazes me is that while time after time I failed you, God, you never failed me. With every step you loved me, guided me, and held me as you wiped away my tears and taught me what true happiness looks like. And for that, I am forever grateful to you. After all, true happiness is only found *in* you.

To Mom and Dad, Rosemarie and Donald Crabtree, you both are not only the greatest parents in the world but the ultimate example of God's warriors fighting the good fight of faith and winning. Thank you for bringing the Word of God to life through your daily example of genuine dependence on our heavenly Father. On behalf of all your children—Glenn, Julie, Shawn, Mindi, and myself—thank you for being our prayer warriors, our champions, our encouragers, our comedy relief, our support, and our perfect examples of how to talk ourselves happy with the heart and Word of God no matter what life throws at us.

To my siblings, especially Shawn and Mindi, thank you for your friendship and counsel. Thank you for hours of phone calls where you allowed me to vent, scream, cry, laugh, and grow.

To God's hand-picked prayer warriors who prayed me out of the ditches of doubt, despair, and discouragement, I thank you. I'm certain God assigned innumerable individuals to pray for me that I am unaware of. To all those unknown faces, I appreciate you more than you could ever imagine. Your prayers worked. To those special faces I know and whose hearts have linked with mine, I give you a special thanks. Dr. Shailja Collins, my sister in Christ and true friend. Your weekly phone calls and hours of praying for me when all I could do was cry on the other end of the phone were more priceless to me than gold. To Bishop Neville Smith, my Bermudian partner in crime, and to Ivorie Anthony who always appeared at my front door at the right time. Thank you all for loving me enough to use your words to lift me up and to speak strength back into my being.

To my sister friend who both looks and acts more like a sister than a friend, Michelle McKinney Hammond. Thank you so much for pushing me forward and supporting me when so many others left me.

To Tony and Monica Beyer, you both have exemplary hearts of service for God. Words can never express how much I appreciated your calls, the cards, the gifts, and the constant words of encouragement. I was but a stranger, and you made Chase and me a part of your family. Thank you!

To Crissy Talbot White. You are the essence of service, kindness, compassion, diligence, faith, discipline, and good ole fashion caring. Thank you for listening to God and sacrificing your time, money, and energy to help me when I needed it the most—never expecting anything in return. Crissy, you showed me what sacrificial friendship looks like. Girl, you're the bomb! And the best fitness trainer out there to boot!

To my southern friend dear to my heart, Kursti Woolard. Girl, from the moment you stepped into my life, you made it better. Thank you for your help, your heart for God, and your southern hospitality. You make things happen and you get things done and I love you for it. Thank you for being my friend and for allowing me to be me.

To my literary agent, Teresa Evenson at the William K. Jensen Literary Agency. Thank you for dealing with my *crazy* when I was still trying to find my "happy."

To Jessica Wong at Nelson Books, girl, you're a miracle worker. I can't thank you enough for working with me and bringing out the best in this book. You are the bomb! Go ahead, say it! And thank you to the Thomas Nelson team. Everyone who had a hand in the production of this book, I applaud you and appreciate your excellence.

And last but most certainly not least. A special thanks to Chase Watts. My son. You are the love of my life, the light within my heart, and the brightness that illuminates my smile. Thank you for making me a better person. Thank you for making me laugh. And thank you for making me happy.

Scripture Wrap

Talk Yourself Happy is about encouraging yourself with the Word of God. But before we can expect God to transform our hearts with his endless promises, we must first make sure that we invite the One who holds our promises into our hearts. Jesus Christ.

"The word is near you; it is in your mouth and in your heart," that is, the message concerning faith that we proclaim: *If you declare with your mouth, "Jesus is Lord," and believe in your heart that God raised him from the dead, you will be saved.* For it is with your heart that you believe and are justified, and it is with your mouth that you profess your faith and are saved. (Romans 10:8–10)

As you think about the handprint of God on your life, take this time to talk to him by asking him to come into your heart. Ask him to take over your life by guiding you with his loving hand. And ask him to fill you with his immeasurable love and joy that encompass his presence. Here's a prayer you can speak out loud.

Lord,

I ask you to come into my heart. I confess with my mouth and believe in my heart that you are Lord. You are the Son of God, and you died on the cross for my sins and rose from the dead to save me, to make me new, and to give me eternal life in your everlasting love. Jesus, I ask you to forgive me for all my sins and from this day on, I commit my life to you, your Word, and your love.

In Jesus' name, amen.

There's no better joy than knowing that God sees his children, hears us, and actively interacts with us through the power of his Word, which reveals his love for us. Every day we've got to remind ourselves who God is and remember that God is greater than any issue, challenge, or lie the enemy throws at us. The key is to hold on to the Word and continually speak God's Word of truth over our lives.

True transformation can only be obtained by the power of the Holy Spirit. When I was younger, I thought we had to fast, pray, and pretty much beg God to fill us with the Holy Spirit. But Scripture tells us that the Holy Spirit isn't earned by our efforts but instead is a *gift* from God. And just as we obtain the gift of salvation by asking Jesus into our hearts, we obtain the gift of the Holy Spirit in the same way. It's as simple as asking, believing, and receiving.

The Holy Spirit allows the Word of God to become alive within our hearts and illuminate areas that are broken, wounded, and hardened so that through the Word, Jesus can heal, restore, and make us pliable to the ways of God. The gift of the Holy Spirit pulls us out of our old selves and ushers us into our new selves.

So I say to you: *Ask* and it will be given to you; *seek* and you will find; *knock* and the door will be opened to you. For everyone who asks receives; the one who seeks finds; and to the one who knocks, the door will be opened. Which of you fathers, if your son asks for a fish, will give him a snake instead? Or if he asks for an egg, will give him a scorpion? If you then, though you are evil, know how to give good gifts to your children, how much more will *your Father in heaven give the Holy Spirit to those who ask him!* (Luke 11:9–13)

It's as simple as asking God to fill you with the Holy Spirit so that God can guide you in all truth and power through his Word.

Following are just a few scriptures you can read, recite, and memorize to build your faith, encourage your heart, and learn how to *talk yourself happy*!

CHAPTER 1: COMPASSION

Colossians 3:12–14

Therefore, as God's chosen people, holy and dearly loved, clothe yourselves with compassion, kindness, humility, gentleness and patience. Bear with each other and forgive one another if any of you has a grievance against someone. Forgive as the Lord forgave you. And over all these virtues put on love, which binds them all together in perfect unity.

1 Thessalonians 5:11–14

Therefore encourage one another and build each other up, just as in fact you are doing. Now we ask you, brothers and sisters, to acknowledge those who work hard among you, who care for you in the Lord and who admonish you. Hold them in the highest regard in love because of their work. Live in peace with each other. And we urge you, brothers and sisters, warn those who are idle and disruptive, encourage the disheartened, help the weak, be patient with everyone.

Romans 12:12–15

Be joyful in hope, patient in affliction, faithful in prayer. Share with the Lord's people who are in need. Practice hospitality. Bless those who persecute you; bless and do not curse. Rejoice with those who rejoice; mourn with those who mourn.

Romans 14:12–13

So then, each of us will give an account of ourselves to God. Therefore let us stop passing judgment on one another. Instead, make up your mind not to put any stumbling block or obstacle in the way of a brother or sister.

Romans 12:16–18

Live in harmony with one another. Do not be proud, but be willing to associate with people of low position. Do not be conceited. Do not repay anyone evil for evil. Be careful to do what is right in the eyes of everyone. If it is possible, as far as it depends on you, live at peace with everyone.

CHAPTER 2: TRUST

Proverbs 3:5–6 NKJV

Trust in the LORD with all your heart,

And lean not on your own understanding;

In all your ways acknowledge Him,

And He shall direct your paths.

Jeremiah 17:7–8

But blessed is the one who trusts in the LORD, whose confidence is in him. They will be like a tree planted by the water that sends out its roots by the stream. It does not fear when heat comes; its leaves are always green. It has no worries in a year of drought and never fails to bear fruit.

Psalm 37:4–6 NKJV

Delight yourself also in the LORD,

And He shall give you the desires of your heart.

Commit your way to the LORD,

Trust also in Him,

And He shall bring it to pass.

He shall bring forth your righteousness as the light,

And your justice as the noonday.

Psalm 46:10 NKJV

> Be still, and know that I am God;
> I will be exalted among the nations,
> I will be exalted in the earth!

Matthew 6:25-27

"Therefore I tell you, do not worry about your life, what you will eat or drink; or about your body, what you will wear. Is not life more than food, and the body more than clothes? Look at the birds of the air; they do not sow or reap or store away in barns, and yet your heavenly Father feeds them. Are you not much more valuable than they? Can any one of you by worrying add a single hour to your life?"

Psalm 9:10

> Those who know your name trust in you,
>> for you, LORD, have never forsaken those who seek you.

Hebrews 11:6

And without faith it is impossible to please God, because anyone who comes to him must believe that he exists and that he rewards those who earnestly seek him.

Psalm 40:1-3

> I waited patiently for the LORD;
>> he turned to me and heard my cry.
> He lifted me out of the slimy pit,
>> out of the mud and mire;

he set my feet on a rock
and gave me a firm place to stand.
He put a new song in my mouth,
a hymn of praise to our God.
Many will see and fear the LORD
and put their trust in him.

CHAPTER 3: IDENTITY

2 Corinthians 5:20-21

We are therefore Christ's ambassadors, as though God were making his appeal through us. We implore you on Christ's behalf: Be reconciled to God. God made him who had no sin to be sin for us, so that in him we might become the righteousness of God.

Colossians 3:12-14

Therefore, as God's chosen people, holy and dearly loved, clothe yourselves with compassion, kindness, humility, gentleness and patience. Bear with each other and forgive one another if any of you has a grievance against someone. Forgive as the Lord forgave you. And over all these virtues put on love, which binds them all together in perfect unity. [Continue reading the chapter; it's good!]

Romans 12:1-2

Therefore, I urge you, brothers and sisters, in view of God's mercy, to offer your bodies as a living sacrifice, holy and pleasing to God—this is your true and proper worship. Do not conform to the pattern of this world, but be transformed by the renewing of your mind. Then you will be able to test and approve what God's will is—his good, pleasing and perfect will.

2 Corinthians 5:17–19

Therefore, if anyone is in Christ, the new creation has come: The old has gone, the new is here! All this is from God, who reconciled us to himself through Christ and gave us the ministry of reconciliation: that God was reconciling the world to himself in Christ, not counting people's sins against them. And he has committed to us the message of reconciliation.

1 Corinthians 6:12–20

"I have the right to do anything," you say—but not everything is beneficial. "I have the right to do anything"—but I will not be mastered by anything. You say, "Food for the stomach and the stomach for food, and God will destroy them both." The body, however, is not meant for sexual immorality but for the Lord, and the Lord for the body. By his power God raised the Lord from the dead, and he will raise us also. Do you not know that your bodies are members of Christ himself? Shall I then take the members of Christ and unite them with a prostitute? Never! Do you not know that he who unites himself with a prostitute is one with her in body? For it is said, "The two will become one flesh." But whoever is united with the Lord is one with him in spirit.

Flee from sexual immorality. All other sins a person commits are outside the body, but whoever sins sexually, sins against their own body. Do you not know that your bodies are temples of the Holy Spirit, who is in you, whom you have received from God? You are not your own; you were bought at a price. Therefore honor God with your bodies.

CHAPTER 4: OBEDIENCE

1 John 5:3-5

In fact, this is love for God: to keep his commands. And his commands are not burdensome, for everyone born of God overcomes the world. This is the victory that has overcome the world, even our faith. Who is it that overcomes the world? Only the one who believes that Jesus is the Son of God.

James 1:22-25

Do not merely listen to the word, and so deceive yourselves. Do what it says. Anyone who listens to the word but does not do what it says is like someone who looks at his face in a mirror and, after looking at himself, goes away and immediately forgets what he looks like. But whoever looks intently into the perfect law that gives freedom, and continues in it—not forgetting what they have heard, but doing it—they will be blessed in what they do.

Proverbs 3:1-4

My son, do not forget my teaching,
    but keep my commands in your heart,
for they will prolong your life many years
    and bring you peace and prosperity.

Let love and faithfulness never leave you;
    bind them around your neck,
    write them on the tablet of your heart.
Then you will win favor and a good name
    in the sight of God and man.

Philippians 1:9–11

And this is my prayer: that your love may abound more and more in knowledge and depth of insight, so that you may be able to discern what is best and may be pure and blameless for the day of Christ, filled with the fruit of righteousness that comes through Jesus Christ—to the glory and praise of God.

Luke 10:27

"Love the Lord your God with all your heart and with all your soul and with all your strength and with all your mind"; and, "Love your neighbor as yourself."

Deuteronomy 28:1–2

If you fully obey the LORD your God and carefully follow all his commands I give you today, the LORD your God will set you high above all the nations on earth. All these blessings will come on you and accompany you if you obey the LORD your God.

Jeremiah 7:23 ESV

But this command I gave them: "Obey my voice, and I will be your God, and you shall be my people. And walk in all the way that I command you, that it may be well with you."

CHAPTER 5: FORGIVENESS

Mark 11:25

And when you stand praying, if you hold anything against anyone, forgive them, so that your Father in heaven may forgive you your sins.

Ephesians 4:32

Be kind and compassionate to one another, forgiving each other, just as in Christ God forgave you.

1 John 1:9

If we confess our sins, he is faithful and just and will forgive us our sins and purify us from all unrighteousness.

James 5:16

Therefore confess your sins to each other and pray for each other so that you may be healed. The prayer of a righteous person is powerful and effective.

Luke 6:27-28

Love your enemies, do good to those who hate you, bless those who curse you, pray for those who mistreat you.

Luke 6:37

Do not judge, and you will not be judged. Do not condemn, and you will not be condemned. Forgive, and you will be forgiven.

Proverbs 10:12

> Hatred stirs up conflict,
>> but love covers over all wrongs.

2 Corinthians 2:5–8 ESV

> Now if anyone has caused pain, he has caused it not to me, but in some measure—not to put it too severely—to all of you. For such a one, this punishment by the majority is enough, so you should rather turn to forgive and comfort him, or he may be overwhelmed by excessive sorrow. So I beg you to reaffirm your love for him.

CHAPTER 6: PRAISE

Psalm 103:1–5

> Praise the LORD, my soul;
>> all my inmost being, praise his holy name.
> Praise the LORD, my soul,
>> and forget not all his benefits—
> who forgives all your sins
>> and heals all your diseases,
> who redeems your life from the pit
>> and crowns you with love and compassion,
> who satisfies your desires with good things
>> so that your youth is renewed like the eagle's.

Psalm 100:1–5 ESV

>Make a joyful noise to the Lord, all the earth!
>>Serve the Lord with gladness!
>>Come into his presence with singing!

>Know that the Lord, he is God!
>>It is he who made us, and we are his;
>>we are his people, and the sheep of his pasture.

>Enter his gates with thanksgiving,
>>and his courts with praise!
>>Give thanks to him; bless his name!

>For the Lord is good;
>>his steadfast love endures forever,
>>and his faithfulness to all generations.

Psalm 28:7

>The Lord is my strength and my shield;
>>my heart trusts in him, and he helps me.
>My heart leaps for joy,
>>and with my song I praise him.

Psalm 117:1–2 ESV

>Praise the Lord, all nations!
>>Extol him, all peoples!
>For great is his steadfast love toward us,
>>and the faithfulness of the Lord endures forever.
>Praise the Lord!

Zephaniah 3:17 ESV

> The LORD your God is in your midst,
>> a mighty one who will save;
> he will rejoice over you with gladness;
>> he will quiet you by his love;
> he will exult over you with loud singing.

Colossians 3:16 ESV

> Let the word of Christ dwell in you richly, teaching and admonishing one another in all wisdom, singing psalms and hymns and spiritual songs, with thankfulness in your hearts to God.

Psalm 34:1–5

> I will extol the LORD at all times;
>> his praise will always be on my lips.
> I will glory in the LORD;
>> let the afflicted hear and rejoice.
> Glorify the LORD with me;
>> let us exalt his name together.

> I sought the LORD, and he answered me;
>> he delivered me from all my fears.
> Those who look to him are radiant;
>> their faces are never covered with shame.

CHAPTER 7: HELP

Romans 12:9–13

Love must be sincere. Hate what is evil; cling to what is good. Be devoted to one another in love. Honor one another above yourselves. Never be lacking in zeal, but keep your spiritual fervor, serving the Lord. Be joyful in hope, patient in affliction, faithful in prayer. Share with the Lord's people who are in need. Practice hospitality.

1 John 3:17–18

If anyone has material possessions and sees a brother or sister in need but has no pity on them, how can the love of God be in that person? Dear children, let us not love with words or speech but with actions and in truth.

Isaiah 41:10

So do not fear, for I am with you;
  do not be dismayed, for I am your God.
I will strengthen you and help you;
  I will uphold you with my righteous right hand.

1 Peter 4:10

Each of you should use whatever gift you have received to serve others, as faithful stewards of God's grace in its various forms.

Proverbs 19:17 ESV

Whoever is generous to the poor lends to the LORD,
  and he will repay him for his deed.

James 2:14–17

What good is it, my brothers and sisters, if someone claims to have faith but has no deeds? Can such faith save them? Suppose a brother or a sister is without clothes and daily food. If one of you says to them, "Go in peace; keep warm and well fed," but does nothing about their physical needs, what good is it? In the same way, faith by itself, if it is not accompanied by action, is dead.

CHAPTER 8: PROMISE

Jeremiah 29:11

"For I know the plans I have for you," declares the LORD, "plans to prosper you and not to harm you, plans to give you hope and a future."

John 15:7–8 ESV

If you abide in me, and my words abide in you, ask whatever you wish, and it will be done for you. By this my Father is glorified, that you bear much fruit and so prove to be my disciples.

Galatians 6:9

Let us not become weary in doing good, for at the proper time we will reap a harvest if we do not give up.

Luke 10:19

I have given you authority to trample on snakes and scorpions and to overcome all the power of the enemy; nothing will harm you.

Isaiah 54:17 NKJV

"No weapon formed against you shall prosper,
And every tongue which rises against you in judgment
You shall condemn.
This is the heritage of the servants of the LORD,
And their righteousness is from Me,"
Says the LORD.

Philippians 4:19–20

And my God will meet all your needs according to the riches of his glory in Christ Jesus. To our God and Father be glory for ever and ever. Amen.

Romans 15:13

May the God of hope fill you with all joy and peace as you trust in him, so that you may overflow with hope by the power of the Holy Spirit.

Ephesians 3:20–21

Now to him who is able to do immeasurably more than all we ask or imagine, according to his power that is at work within us, to him be glory in the church and in Christ Jesus throughout all generations, for ever and ever! Amen.

2 Corinthians 1:20

For no matter how many promises God has made, they are "Yes" in Christ. And so through him the "Amen" is spoken by us to the glory of God.

Psalm 9:10

> Those who know your name trust in you,
>
>> for you, Lord, have never forsaken those who seek you.

Hebrews 11:6

> And without faith it is impossible to please God, because anyone who comes to him must believe that he exists and that he rewards those who earnestly seek him.

Psalm 40:1-3

> I waited patiently for the Lord;
>
>> he turned to me and heard my cry.
>
> He lifted me out of the slimy pit,
>
>> out of the mud and mire;
>
> he set my feet on a rock
>
>> and gave me a firm place to stand.
>
> He put a new song in my mouth,
>
>> a hymn of praise to our God.
>
> Many will see and fear the Lord
>
>> and put their trust in him.

About the Author

Kristi Watts is best known for her role as a former cohost on the award-winning television program *The 700 Club* and for her in-depth interviews with authors, celebrities, and public figures such as former secretary of state Condoleezza Rice and movie mogul Tyler Perry. She recently launched Kristi Watts Ministries to provide Bible study tools, video blogs, and speaking engagements. Kristi lives in Virginia Beach, Virginia, with her son.

www.KristiWattsMinistries.com